creation points

Darwin and Darwinism 150 years later:

Biblical faith and the Christian worldview

Ian McNaughton and Paul Taylor   DayOne

© Day One Publications 2009
First printed 2009

ISBN 978–1–84625–162–7

British Library Cataloguing in Publication Data available

Published by Day One Publications
Ryelands Road, Leominster, HR6 8NZ
☎ 01568 613 740 FAX 01568 611 473
email—sales@dayone.co.uk
web site—www.dayone.co.uk
North American—e-mail—sales@dayonebookstore.com
North American—web site—www.dayonebookstore.com

Answers in Genesis
PO Box 8078, Leicester, LE21 9AJ
0116 270 8400
ptaylor@answersingenesis.org
Answers in Genesis (the ministry of Creation Science Foundation) is a non-profit, Christ-centred, non-denominational, evangelistic ministry dedicated to upholding the authority of the Bible from the very first verse.

Cover design by Wayne McMaster
Printed by Gutenberg Press, Malta

In this book, Paul Taylor and Ian McNaughton show how the evolutionary philosophy changed the scientific outlook and paradigm of the nineteenth and twentieth centuries. What they also show is the movement away from solid foundations in Darwin's ancestors, who were heavily influenced by Unitarianism, and then in Darwin's life to a movement right away from trust in the authority of God's Word. Evolutionary thinking was spawned in unbelief, and only by a return to a biblical creation viewpoint can we again understand properly the message of the Scriptures and the teaching of the Fall and redemption.

Andy McIntosh DSc, FIMA, CMath, FEI, CEng, FInstP, MIGEM, FRAeS, Professor of Thermodynamics and Combustion Theory, University of Leeds, and author of Genesis for Today

This excellent book clearly explains how Darwin's humanistic worldview, rather than scientific evidence, was the main motivating factor behind the theory of evolution. The book also explains how theistic evolution is not a reconciliation of science with the Bible but rather a damaging union of humanism and the Bible.

Stuart Burgess, Professor of Design and Nature, UK, and author of Hallmarks of Design

I thank God for AIG, and for their steadfast stand against the ever-increasing rabbit trails of Darwinian imagineers.

Ray Comfort, CEO of Living Waters Ministries, California, and author of The Way of the Master

To the growing bank of literature exposing the flaws in Darwinian evolution, this small and accessible book is a valuable contribution. A plain and potent critique of Darwinianism, together with the careless views held by some Christians that it has spawned, is woven into a thoroughly reasonable alternative based upon the authority of the Bible—and one that does not conflict with good science.

Brian H. Edwards, author, speaker, and former president of the Fellowship of Independent Evangelical Churches

Commendations

My colleagues Ian and Paul share my burden to reach Darwin's homeland with the life-changing creation/gospel message. May God bless their effort to show Britons—and others who read this book—that God's Word is accurate and authoritative in our modern-day society.

Ken Ham, President, Answers in Genesis/Creation Museum, USA

While Misters Dawkins, Hitchins and Harris bankroll millions selling anger, Darwin and Darwinism *lays out the level-headed truth, at a fraction of the price.*

Todd Friel, presenter of Wretched Radio (www.wretchedradio.com)

In the debate about origins, Christianity is pitted against science. This has not always been the case; however, there has been a constant tension between faith and unbelief, and now that the new Darwinism treats Charles Darwin as a messiah, this tension has broken out into 'war'. One only needs to listen to the comments of leading British atheists and academics such as Professors Steve Jones and Richard Dawkins to realize their profound esteem for the naturalist and their intense disrespect for all things biblical. They are not alone. At the Natural History Museum in London, Darwin's marble statue has replaced that of Sir Richard Owen (the museum's founder) on the landing of its Central Hall because Darwin is now regarded as the hero who has delivered science from the 'tyranny' and perceived ignorance of the Holy Scriptures and the Christian church. That Charles Darwin is esteemed today as the saviour of science and sage of modernity is, of course, nonsense, but to listen to his disciples, one would think that evolution was unknown and unheard of before the book *On the Origin of Species* was printed and that Darwin received his ideas from heaven (if they believe in heaven) like some esteemed prophet of old. If they are right, it would make Charles Darwin greater than Jesus Christ, the founder and prophet of Christianity, who obviously accepted the Genesis account of creation as true.

This book happily accepts the usefulness of empirical science in all scientific disciplines but rejects the approach to science that is more 'faith'-based than evidence-based; as one author has said, 'It is fundamental to realize that science cannot prove how the universe began. Human observation, either directly through the senses or indirectly through scientific instruments, is the foundation and prerequisite for establishing scientific proof.'[1] For this reason, creationist evangelicals treat the evolutionary hypothesis as having no verifiable scientific basis. Creationists and evolutionists have the same evidence, yet neither can go back and scientifically repeat the origin of the universe in a laboratory; all they can do is look at the evidence and, depending on their worldviews, draw conclusions. Either view must be accepted on faith. We openly state that the views expressed in this small book are grounded in the belief that the sixty-six books that make up the Bible, as given by divine revelation and transmitted to the church, are without error (2 Tim. 3:16).

Evolutionary naturalists, such as David Attenborough, have tried to convince us that animals and plants, large and small—whether evolved or created—have the ability to change themselves into survivors. Species do change, but it is biologically impossible for the 'kinds' created by God to change into other species because the genetic information is not present to enable this to happen. Paul Garner has said,

Darwin corrected a popular misunderstanding. Species do change. Since Darwin's day many observations have confirmed this ... [and] contrary to the accepted wisdom of Darwin's day the Bible nowhere teaches that species are fixed and unchanging (in fact it does not even use the word *species*). Rather, the Book of Genesis refers to 'kinds' (Gen. 1:11, 21) and suggests that living things have their own dynamic history. While Darwin was right to argue that species change, he went too far. He should have gone back to Scripture to see what it really said.[2]

Evolutionists fail to see that this ability to survive, and to change within kinds, was in God's plan all along so that life could cope with the harsh conditions that would result as a consequence of the Fall in the Garden of Eden.

Believing that the earth and the universe are several thousand years old is not fashionable today, but as evangelical Christians we are committed to trusting the Bible from the very first verse in Genesis 1. We know that many in the institutional churches are falling under the sway of naturalism and the new Darwinism. This includes the Roman Catholic Church, which has now succumbed to the view that a theistic evolutionary hypothesis is acceptable. The Roman see should know better, but it appears to have repeated the errors of its past and is continuing to place Roman tradition and dogma before the holy and inerrant Scriptures. Creationists believe that God created a mature universe *ex nihilo* (out of nothing).

The culture of teaching evolution in our schools as fact has resulted in the church's children being stolen from them through unbelief; even for children at the young age of ten years old, this is a reality. With this in mind, and with the knowledge that the national culture is changing under the influence of atheism and secularism, and because of the failure of the churches to teach and preach the Word of God as truth for every generation, we write this book with the prayer that it will contribute to the reviving of true religion in the UK and beyond. What needs to be grasped by Christians is that 'we do not wrestle against flesh and blood, but against principalities, against powers … against spiritual hosts of wickedness in the heavenly places' (Eph. 6:12).

Notes

1 **B. G. Ranganathan,** *Origins* (Edinburgh: Banner of Truth, 1988), pp. 2–3.
2 **Paul Garner,** 'Do Species Change?', in *Answers*, 4/1 (2009), pp. 36–39.

Contents

Before Darwin

Where were you when I laid the foundations of the earth? Tell Me, if you have understanding. (Job 38:4)

E volution has a long history. Ideas of evolution predate Darwin by millennia. It is not too much of an exaggeration to suggest that many prevailing forms of opposition to biblical Christianity are evolutionary in nature.

The worst sort of delusion is self-delusion. The oldest self-delusion reported is that of the devil, who convinced himself that he could become like God:

For you have said in your heart:
'I will ascend into heaven,
I will exalt my throne above the stars of God;
I will also sit on the mount of the congregation
On the farthest sides of the north;
I will ascend above the heights of the clouds,
I will be like the Most High.'
(Isa. 14:13–14)

This verse is part of a passage about the king of Babylon (Isa. 14:3–21). However, it is likely that a person other than a human king is also being referred to. Babylon is, after all, used typically elsewhere in Scripture, and this king is said to have 'fallen from heaven' (v. 12). A human king would not have fallen from heaven, so he is being used as a type of the angelic being known as Satan, even if it is a real human king who is being spoken of. In other words, the reference to the king of Babylon could be both real and symbolic. The being referred to in this passage is also named as 'Lucifer' (v. 12; some translations have 'Day Star'). This is the only place in the Bible where the word occurs, but traditionally it has been assumed that Lucifer is simply another name for Satan.

If this is the case, then pride was the source of Satan's sin. His desire was to become like God. But notice how he thought this equality with God could be achieved: he intended it to happen by his ascending above the heights of the clouds. He believed that he could become like God by his own actions. We can therefore also presume that he thought that was how God had achieved his current status. In other words, Satan did not believe that God had always been God, but rather that he had evolved into that position, and, therefore, that maybe he, Satan, could evolve similarly. It is perhaps not too presumptuous to assume that this is the first example of the theory of evolution.

Darwin's ideas had a history

Everybody knows that Charles Darwin sailed around the world on HMS *Beagle*. When the ship got to the Galápagos Islands, Darwin saw different finches on different islands, with different-sized and different-shaped beaks. They could not have been created this way—they must have developed one from another. Therefore, he came to the conclusion that all organisms had developed from other organisms by a process of gradual evolution by natural selection. Everybody knows that Darwin formulated his theory after seeing the irrefutable evidence on his world voyage.

Except that that is not how it happened. Darwin was already convinced of evolution and deep time (long ages) before he even stepped foot on the *Beagle*. Nor was he the first to formulate an evolutionary theory; we have just suggested biblical evidence of evolutionary thinking. In fact, none of Darwin's ideas was even particularly original. As we shall see, he seemed not to be above plagiarism—or, at the very least, reporting on other people's work without sufficient citation or reference.

In our studies of Darwin and the Bible, it will be worth our while examining some of the antecedents of Darwinism and how Darwin's ideas were influenced by others and developed before his famous voyage on the *Beagle*.

Darwin had a grandfather

Darwin actually had two famous grandfathers: Josiah Wedgwood, of pottery fame, was a member of the scientific Lunar Society along with James Watt, who radicalized the design of the steam engine, and Joseph

Erasmus Darwin, Charles's grandfather

Priestley, the famous chemist. Another member of this illustrious society was Erasmus Darwin—Charles's other grandfather.

Erasmus Darwin lived from 1731 to 1802, dying seven years before his famous grandson's birth. He worked as a physician in the Midlands for over fifty years. He wrote and studied widely, publishing works on botany and carrying out experiments with electricity, inventions and rockets. Probably his most important scientific work was *Zoönomia*, in which he anticipated the later evolutionary ideas of Lamarck as well as those of his grandson. Although Charles was born after Erasmus died, it is inconceivable that the younger Darwin was not aware of his grandfather's work.

Note how 'Darwinian' are the views of Erasmus Darwin in this extract from *Zoönomia*:

Would it be too bold to imagine that, in the great length of time since the earth began to exist, perhaps millions of ages before the commencement of the history of mankind, would it be too bold to imagine that all warm-blooded animals have arisen from one living filament, which the great First Cause endued with animality, with the power of acquiring new parts, attended with new propensities, directed by irritations, sensations, volitions and associations, and thus possessing the faculty of continuing to improve by its own inherent activity, and of delivering down these improvements by generation to its posterity, world without end![1]

It will be noticed that the older Darwin believed in millions of years, or at least, long ages. He also believed in common ancestry for warm-blooded animals. He accepted an evolutionary concept of improvement—even though it was more a Lamarckian improvement (see below) than a Darwinian natural selection. He also believed in ages before the (evolutionary) appearance of mankind.

Other Darwin antecedents

Charles Darwin was, therefore, not the originator of evolutionary ideas— nor even of natural selection. Dr David Menton writes as follows:

In today's public schools, history teachers teach how the universe evolved; earth science teachers tell how the earth evolved; biology teachers relate how living things evolved; and social studies teachers preach about how our values and religion evolved—however, students are rarely instructed in how belief in evolutionism itself evolved. To be sure, it didn't begin with Darwin, nor was it first proposed by scientists working in the field or in the laboratory.[2]

Nor was Erasmus Darwin alone in his early evolutionism; he was much influenced in his ideas by James Burnett, Lord Monboddo.

Monboddo (1714–1799) was a Scottish lawyer. His title was not hereditary, being obtained when he became a member of the Judicial Committee of the House of Lords. Monboddo clearly believed in evolution—including a common ancestry for humans and apes. Monboddo's successor at the House of Lords, Charles Neaves, wrote a disparaging poem about Charles Darwin's ideas, claiming that they were stolen from his friend Monboddo.[3] Monboddo's views were considerably less Lamarckian than those of Erasmus Darwin and contained elements of ideas about natural selection. It is also worth noting that Monboddo was a man of some religious faith. He therefore attempted to harmonize Scripture with his evolutionary and deep-time views by insisting that the accounts in the early chapters of Genesis were just allegories. Such compromises in the 18th century were remarkably similar to those of today.

Reference has already been made to French biologist Jean-Baptiste Lamarck (1744–1829). Lamarck is best known today for his evolutionary ideas—most school science textbooks refer to his pre-Darwinian evolutionism, but frequently they do so in a way which implies that he was the only precursor to Darwin—which, as we have seen, is not the case.

Lamarck differed from other scientists in areas other than evolutionary biology. For example, he disagreed with the chemistry of Priestley and Lavoisier, maintaining a belief in the old theories of a four-element universe (earth, water, air, and fire, or phlogiston).

Lamarckian evolution suggested that very simple plants and animals arose by spontaneous generation, while subsequent organisms evolved from these by being modified by circumstances. His idea was that new behaviours, caused by their circumstances, would arise in animals. These behaviours would then be passed on to the next generation.

It is popular for Lamarck's ideas to be scoffed at today. Yet are his ideas of environmental modifications really any less plausible than Darwin's suggestions of natural selection coupled with mutations? Some UK school textbooks even refer to Lamarck with the same sort of condescending disparagement usually reserved for creationists, for example:

The word 'biology' was first invented by Jean-Baptiste Lamarck. He suggested a theory of evolution of animals without backbones (invertebrates) before Charles Darwin. However, his ideas were fundamentally flawed because he believed that evolution occurred because characteristics that were developed during the lifetime of an organism were inherited by its offspring. For example, if Lamarck had been correct, children of well-developed trained weightlifters would always inherit strength and large muscles.4

Lamarck's theory is now discredited ...5

In other areas of science, opposing theories are not treated with such disdain. Yet, in the realm of evolutionary science, any view that diverges from the accepted neo-Darwinian position is treated like a medieval heresy. Note, for example, the put-downs used by arch-Darwinian Richard Dawkins on fellow evolutionary biologist Stephen J. Gould, developer of the alternative *punctuated equilibrium* view of evolution. Dawkins described Gould's work as being filled with 'forced analogies that obscure rather than illuminate' and 'bad scientific poetry'.6 If Darwinians will use such strong language against fellow, but slightly differing, evolutionists, it is small wonder that creationists feel the lash of their tongues.

Hutton and uniformitarianism

James Hutton (1726–1797) formed ideas that were very important antecedents of Darwinism. It was Hutton who developed the concepts of deep time (millions of years of earth history, rather than just thousands) and uniformitarianism (defined below).

The impact of Hutton's ideas can be gauged from this anecdote. Some time ago, one of the authors was travelling around the city of Edinburgh—where Hutton lived and worked—on the open-top deck of a tour bus. As the bus passed Salisbury Crags, the tour guide remarked that it was by looking at these rocks that Hutton first proved the Bible to be wrong.

Salisbury Crags, Edinburgh

Hutton was a bit of a polymath and also a perpetual student. He started his working life as a lawyer, then trained in chemistry, then in medicine, and finally founded a business producing sal ammoniac from coal dust.[7] However, his passion outside of work was geology. When he observed rock formations, such as those at Salisbury Crags, or at Siccar Point, a few kilometres east of Edinburgh, he decided that he could explain the rock formations as having occurred over vast periods of time. His observation was that changes happen to rocks at a very slow rate. He dismissed the alternative catastrophist views and assumed that these processes had always occurred at this rate. Therefore, he surmised that the rock structures were very old. This gave rise to the concept of deep time—although Hutton did not believe that the earth was millions of years old. In fact, he believed that the earth was of infinite age, and that these slow processes had always been happening. His views gave rise to what is known as *uniformitarianism*: the belief that processes measured today must have been proceeding at the same rate in the past. This concept was summed up by Charles Lyell with the telling phrase 'the present is the key to the past'. It is not too much of an exaggeration to suggest that uniformitarianism is mentioned in Scripture:

... knowing this first: that scoffers will come in the last days, walking according to their own lusts, and saying, 'Where is the promise of His coming? For since the fathers fell asleep, all things continue as they were from the beginning of creation.' For this they willfully forget: that by the word of God the heavens were of old, and the earth standing out of water and in the water, by which the world that then existed perished, being flooded with water. (2 Peter 3:3–6)

The uniformitarianism is expressed by the scoffers' comment 'all things continue as they were from the beginning of creation'. The refutation of uniformitarianism is based on the fact that it ignores two huge events in world history—the creation and the Flood. Once these are factored into the equation, all results interpreted by uniformitarianism are open to re-interpretation.

Hutton was not content to restrict his uniformitarianism to geology. He began to apply these assumptions to biology as well. His views could therefore be described as evolutionary, as seen in the following quote:

If an organized body is not in the situation and circumstances best adapted to its sustenance and propagation, then, in conceiving an indefinite variety among the individuals of that species, we must be assured, that, on the one hand, those which depart most from the best adapted constitution, will be the most liable to perish, while, on the other hand, those organized bodies, which most approach to the best constitution for the present circumstances, will be best adapted to continue, in preserving themselves and multiplying the individuals of their race.[8]

Hutton's ideas were of great influence on Charles Lyell, and Lyell, as we shall see later, had a great influence on Charles Darwin. All the ideas of the above men—and of others who lived and worked during Darwin's lifetime—constitute a filter through which the emergence of Darwin's evolutionary theory must be understood. Thus the myth that Darwin began life as a Bible-believing Christian and suddenly understood evolution while travelling on the *Beagle* is rather far from the truth. Darwin's ideas were already in embryo before he reached the Galápagos Islands, and evolutionary and naturalistic influences were already in place before the *Beagle* left Plymouth.

Notes

1 **Erasmus Darwin,** *Zoönomia*, 1796, at: gutenberg.org/files/15707/15707-h/15707-h.htm.

2 **David Menton,** 'The Origin of Evolutionism: It Didn't Begin with Darwin', 1995, at: gennet.org/facts/metro21.html.

3 **Charles Neaves,** *Songs and Verses* (4th edn.; London, 1875), p. 5.

4 **P. Barratt et al.,** *WJEC GCSE Science and GCSE Additional Science* (London: Hodder Murray, 2006), p. 16.

5 **B. Dawson et al.,** *OCR Science for GCSE (Gateway Science)* (Oxford: Heinemann, 2006), p. 62.

6 Quoted in **R. McKie,** 'Doctor Zoo', *The Observer*, 25 July 2004.

7 'James Hutton', *Encyclopaedia Britannica*, at: britannica.com.

8 Quoted in **Paul Pearson,** 'Review of *An Investigation of the Principles of Knowledge and of the Progress of Reason, from Sense to Science and Philosophy* by James Hutton (1794)', *Nature*, 425 (2003), p. 665.

The early years

And these words which I command you today shall be in your heart. You shall teach them diligently to your children, and shall talk of them when you sit in your house, when you walk by the way, when you lie down, and when you rise up. You shall bind them as a sign on your hand, and they shall be as frontlets between your eyes. You shall write them on the doorposts of your house and on your gates. (Deut. 6:6–9)

When all that generation had been gathered to their fathers, another generation arose after them who did not know the LORD nor the work which He had done for Israel. (Judg. 2:10)

Early influences

Shrewsbury, Darwin's birthplace, has a long and exciting history. Founded sometime in the middle of the first millennium, Shrewsbury began life as a centre for the kings of Powys. However, disputes between Welsh and English kingdoms began well before the Norman Conquest, and Offa, king of Mercia, certainly counted Shrewsbury within his realm.

Shrewsbury is associated with many important events. In the 12th century, the town was caught up in the convulsions known as 'The Anarchy', when there was civil war between the forces of Empress Matilda (daughter and heir of King Henry I) and King Stephen (Henry's nephew). In the 13th century, Shrewsbury was taken by Welsh forces under Prince Llewellyn. In the early 15th century, the Battle of Shrewsbury was fought between the armies of King Henry IV and the rebel Henry Hotspur.

Shrewsbury's geography is strategic. It was built in the middle of a long meander of the River Severn, Britain's longest river, and is just 15 km east of the Welsh border.

Darwin Shopping Centre, Shrewsbury

The town has associations with famous people such as Major-General Robert Clive (Clive of India) and poet Samuel Taylor Coleridge. But a quick walk through the town centre will soon inform you as to the identity of Shrewsbury's most famous son. It is Charles Darwin. His name appears around the town centre, most notably in recent times with the new Darwin Shopping Centre.

The main hub of the town of Shrewsbury is almost an island, nearly encircled as it is by the River Severn. The house where the Darwin family lived—The Mount—is situated north of the Old Town, across the bridge known as the Welsh Bridge. Because of the meander of the Severn at this point, the bluff on which the house is situated overlooks another part of the river. It was Darwin's father, Robert Waring Darwin, who had the house built. Robert was a doctor. However, that description is rather like stating that C. S. Lewis was a university lecturer; it merely states what Dr Darwin's main occupation was, not the breadth of his business. In fact, Dr Darwin was literally a capitalist, trading in securities, bonds and mortgages. Only about one third of his income came from his official vocation. In common with most high-ranking members of society, Dr Darwin attended the local Church of England—St Chad's Church.

The Mount house, the Darwin family home

Nevertheless, his views were profoundly pro-liberal, anti-Tory, and, according to Janet Browne—author of an important two-volume biography of Charles Darwin—he was 'at heart probably an atheist'.[1]

It was into these ideas that Charles was born on 12 February 1809. His father's views cannot have been unknown to the young Charles and are as likely as any later influences to have left their mark on his intellectual development.

Charles's mother, Susannah, came from the Wedgwood family. In many ways, Susannah's religious beliefs were possibly even more influential on his development than his father's. In common with most of the rest of the famous pottery family, Susannah was a Unitarian. Taken by his mother, the young Charles attended the Unitarian Church in Shrewsbury—a plaque outside the High Street chapel commemorates this fact. The minister at the time was one Revd George Case, who ran a small school in a property on Claremont Hill. Charles Darwin was enrolled in this school for a year at the age of eight, and it was here that he first developed his interest in natural history, as the students were taken across the road by St Chad's Church to a quarry—now the site of the beautiful Dingle Gardens.

The Unitarian Church in Shrewsbury

Unitarianism

These childhood influences are worth considering further. It has often been wrongly stated that Darwin was brought up in a Bible-believing Christian environment, which he rejected as a result of his scientific findings. Nothing could be further from the truth. In fact, his formative years involved one parent who was nominally Anglican but actually atheist, and another who was Unitarian. He even suggested in his autobiography that his views may have once been orthodox,[2] though this is likely to be hyperbole, bearing in mind his other views at the time and his unorthodox religious background.

A word needs to be said about Unitarianism. Unitarianism is not simply a rejection of the deity of Jesus Christ. That rejection stems, not from an aberrant interpretation of the scriptural text, but rather from a rejection of the entire authority of that text. The Unitarian attitude to the Bible, for example, is ably expounded by Cliff Reed in his booklet *Unitarian? What's That?* as follows: 'Anything in the Bible that Unitarians accept as true is accepted because it rings true in our own humble reflection upon it. We do not accept it just because it is in the Bible.'[3]

This attitude does not, in fact, reflect humility. Rather, it reflects the

Revd Case's school

opinion of Unitarians that their cogitation on the Bible is of greater benefit than the actual words of Scripture themselves. It sets their own intellects on a higher plane than that of the inspiration of God. Far from humility, this is arrogance. This rejection of scriptural authority has been a hallmark of Unitarianism since its foundation. And it was this religious background which was the primary spiritual influence on the young Darwin as he grew up in the home and in the school, and as he began to take an interest in natural history.

In a comment on human nature, Reed says this: 'Unitarians take a scientific and evolutionary view of human origins. We regard the biblical creation stories as myths.'[4] This is hardly orthodox Christian belief. Now, clearly we must accept that Reed's booklet was written many, many years after Darwin's *Descent of Man* was published, and that Unitarianism—like many other religious groups—has modified and 'evolved' its teachings over the years. Nevertheless, the Unitarianism of Darwin's day would not have accepted the necessity of believing the truth of Genesis any more than would the Unitarianism of today.

This important point cannot be overemphasized. Neither from his father nor his mother did the young Charles Darwin receive biblical

Christian influences. From neither side was there pressure or inclination to believe the Bible's account of creation in Genesis—nor even to believe anything in the Bible. Bearing in mind the backgrounds of both paternal and maternal families, it is also clear that a rejection of biblical Christianity was in no way unusual for the day. Thus the myth that Darwin was somehow an evangelical Christian who lost his faith because he found science is, at best, naïve.

As we have seen, Darwin's interest in natural history began as he attended Revd Case's school. This extract from his autobiography ably illustrates that fact—and also interestingly gives us an insight into a dishonesty in the child:

One little event during this year has fixed itself very firmly in my mind, and I hope that it has done so from my conscience having been afterwards sorely troubled by it; it is curious as showing that apparently I was interested at this early age in the variability of plants! I told another little boy (I believe it was Leighton, who afterwards became a well-known Lichenologist and botanist) that I could produce variously coloured Polyanthuses and Primroses by watering them with certain coloured fluids, which was of course a monstrous fable, and had never been tried by me. I may here also confess that as a little boy I was much given to inventing deliberate falsehoods, and this was always done for the sake of causing excitement. For instance, I once gathered much valuable fruit from my Father's trees and hid them in the shrubbery, and then ran in breathless haste to spread the news that I had discovered a hoard of stolen fruit.[5]

Shrewsbury School

Darwin's idyllic time at Case's school was not to last for long. In July 1817—just a few months after he had started at the school—his mother, Susannah, died. In September 1818, the nine-year-old was sent to board at Shrewsbury School—a famous school run by Revd Dr Samuel Butler, the grandfather of the author of the same name. The unpleasant Dr Skinner of Roughborough School in Butler's *The Way of all Flesh* was based on the author's grandfather. This was certainly the end of the happier part of Darwin's childhood. As Browne has noted, 'The impact of this formal divorce from home can hardly be overestimated. Though the school was a mere fifteen minutes away from home, it might as well have been in another country.'[6] We can only guess at how the trauma of recent bereavement, added to his unhappiness at Shrewsbury School, contributed to Darwin's lack of application at the school.

Dr Butler's education regime clearly did not fit with Darwin's interest in natural history. He complained in his autobiography that the school concentrated on classics, geography and history—all subjects that interested Darwin not at all. 'The school as a means of education to me was simply a blank.'[7] It would appear that there was little to show in the way of educational influence from the years spent at Shrewsbury School. A greater scientific influence was likely to have been the time spent by Darwin with his father in their gardens, where Dr Darwin would often read from scientific works, including those of Darwin's grandfather, Erasmus Darwin, together with the evolutionary ideas contained therein. Other aspects of Darwin's informal, unofficial education are illustrated by the chemistry 'laboratory' set up by Darwin's older brother—also called Erasmus—in the garden tool-house. Charles's interest in scientific experimentation was criticized by the unsympathetic Dr Butler, for his 'wasting time on such useless subjects'[8]. Butler referred to him as a *poco curante*—a Latinized insult of the sort that would be frowned upon in today's educational world.

Despite their apparent closeness, even Dr Darwin got exasperated with Charles's apparent lack of application at school. When he was fifteen, his father, in a temper, exploded, 'You care for nothing but shooting, dogs, and rat-catching, and you will be a disgrace to yourself and all your family.'[9] Dr Darwin felt that he had to remove his son from the school because of his idleness.

Edinburgh

Later that year, in October 1825, Dr Darwin sent the sixteen-year-old Charles to the University of Edinburgh to study for medicine. He took up lodgings with his brother Erasmus in Lothian Street, opposite the university. Erasmus had, by now, almost completed his medical studies. Charles did not take to his medical studies any more than he had enjoyed the classics. He did not enjoy anatomy—or at least, he did not enjoy lectures on it, but he believed that the practice of anatomy might have been more worthwhile for him: 'It has proved one of the greatest evils in my life that I was not urged to practise dissection, for I should soon have got over my disgust; and the practice would have been invaluable for all my future work.'[10]

That there was a squeamishness in Darwin's character seems undeniable, but, in mitigation, some of his problems were also due to an important and commendable tenderness—as in the case when he had to run out of the operating theatre after having watched a botched operation go wrong. The operation concerned was being carried out on a child. He could not bring himself to attend the operating theatre again, describing the event as haunting him 'for many a long year'.[11]

It should also be said that Darwin was critical of the teaching methods used in the university:

The instruction at Edinburgh was altogether by Lectures, and these were intolerably dull, with the exception of those on chemistry by Hope; but to my mind there are no advantages and many disadvantages in lectures compared with reading. Dr. Duncan's lectures on Materia Medica at 8 o'clock on a winter's morning are something fearful to remember. Dr. Munro made his lectures on human anatomy as dull as he was himself, and the subject disgusted me.[12]

It is clear that Darwin was to learn more from books than lectures for the rest of his life. Contemporary records show that, even during Darwin's medical studies in Edinburgh, he and his brother used the library far more than was average for students of their time.

The brothers were only together at Edinburgh for a year, after which Erasmus's studies came to an end. Darwin's second year appears to have been happier—but even then his education seemed to owe more to what happened outside the university rather than inside. His autobiography talks at length about friends and contemporaries who clearly seemed to have influenced him—though, strangely, he maintains that there was no influence. This unwillingness to acknowledge the influence of others possibly relates to later problems leading up to the publication of *On the Origin of Species* and its various revisions, including charges of plagiarism.

An example of this comes in reference to one of his friends, Dr Grant. He recalls an uncharacteristic burst of enthusiasm from Grant as they went for a walk one day. Grant was enthusing on the subject of Lamarck and his writings on evolution. Darwin maintained that 'I listened in silent astonishment, and as far as I can judge without any effect on my mind'.[13] He followed this comment up with remembering reading his grandfather's views on evolution, which he also maintained was 'without producing any effect on me'.[14] It would seem that we should take such protestations with a very healthy pinch of salt. We have already seen that Darwin was brought up in an atmosphere of liberalism and scepticism. It defies logic to suppose that he did not absorb any of this evolutionism.

Darwin frequently attended meetings of the Plinian Society (a student natural history society at the University of Edinburgh) at this time. Although his autobiography mentions this—together with an amusing anecdote—nothing is said of the influence that the society might have had on him. One biographer has suggested that the meetings of the Plinian Society might have been Darwin's first exposure to anti-Christian sentiments;[15] however, this is unlikely. We have already seen that the atheism of his father, his mother's Unitarianism and his grandfather's evolutionism must all have influenced him. Anti-Christian comments in the Society are likely simply to have reinforced a latent anti-Christian attitude in Darwin's own opinions.

Two other great influences during Darwin's time in Edinburgh need to be noted. The first of these major influences, John Edmonstone, receives surprisingly little attention in Darwin's autobiography; Darwin didn't even name him. Edmonstone was a black slave from Guyana who was brought back to the UK by his master. During his captivity, he was taught taxidermy, a profession at which he became highly skilled. Darwin met him after he was given his freedom, when he was working as a taxidermist for Edinburgh University. Darwin was fascinated by the art, and Edmonstone taught him the skill—a skill that was to be invaluable to Darwin on the *Beagle*.

The second major influence on Darwin at this time was the study of geology, a pastime which, actually, Darwin did not like. He found his formal geological studies boring. 'The sole effect they (Dr Jameson's lectures on Geology) produced on me was the determination never as long as I lived to read a book on Geology or in any way to study the science.'[16] Modern evolutionists can be grateful that Darwin did not stick to this determination. What is clear is that Darwin had learned something about the nature of rocks at Salisbury Crags, outside Edinburgh. It would seem likely that he had heard of James Hutton's deep-age views about the Crags—ideas that were later taken up by Charles Lyell, who was to prove such an influence on Charles Darwin.

These influences notwithstanding, the real educational work at Edinburgh was not to Darwin's liking and he left the university during his second year, in April 1827, never to complete his medical studies. His interests were still somewhat bohemian—he spent a great deal of spare time shooting. In the month after he left Edinburgh, he visited London and then went with his uncle, Josiah Wedgwood (son of the original potter) for a trip to Paris. His father was very disappointed in Charles's attitudes at this time and made arrangements for him to study to become a clergyman.

Notes

1 **Janet Browne,** *Charles Darwin: Voyaging* (London: Pimlico, 2003), p. 9.
2 **Charles Darwin,** *The Autobiography of Charles Darwin, 1809–1882* (Sioux Falls, SD: NuVision, 2007), pp. 81–87.
3 **Cliff Reed,** *Unitarian? What's That?*, at: derbyunitarians.org.uk/unitarian_whats_that.html.
4 Ibid.
5 **Browne,** *Charles Darwin: Voyaging*, p. 23.
6 Ibid.
7 **Darwin,** *Autobiography*, p. 14.
8 **Edward Bagnall Poulton,** 'Charles Darwin and the Theory of Natural Selection' (1896);at: darwin-online.org.uk.
9 Ibid. p. 14.
10 Ibid. p. 16.
11 Letter 445 from Charles Darwin to Emma Wedgwood (later Emma Darwin), 27 November 1838; at: darwinproject.ac.uk.
12 Ibid.
13 **Charles Darwin,** *On the Origin of Species* (Peterborough, Ontario: Broadview Press, 2003), p. 426.
14 **Darwin,** *Autobiography*, p. 49.
15 'Outline of Darwin's College Years', at: aboutdarwin.com/timeline/time_03.html.
16 **Darwin,** *Autobiography*, p. 18.

Years of discovery

Train up a child in the way he should go, and when he is old he will not depart from it. (Prov. 22:6)

Cambridge

Darwin's autobiography suggests that he had to consider for a while whether or not becoming a clergyman was the right course. The truth is that he had little option; Robert Darwin was determined that his younger son should not become a wastrel. As we have seen, Robert Darwin was not a believer, even though he was a formal member of the Church of England. Charles's issues, unsurprisingly, were to do with his beliefs—though his autobiographical statements are somewhat contradictory. At first he admits his doubts: 'I asked for some time to consider, as from what little I had heard or thought on the subject I had scruples about declaring my belief in all the dogmas of the Church of England.'[1] Why should he not have had such scruples, given that he was brought up with such a sceptical background? Interestingly, his main attraction to the idea of becoming a clergyman was nothing to do with faith: 'I liked the thought of being a country clergyman.'[2] Yet his scruples were then contradicted by his statement that 'I did not then in the least doubt the strict and literal truth of every word in the Bible'.[3] This statement is very implausible, given the aforementioned influences of his father, mother and grandfather, as well as the formative influence of the Plinian Society. It is likely that Darwin had to make such a comment retrospectively, to justify how his views were later to alter. It is more likely that his religious views, or lack of them, never really significantly changed. It was not uncommon then—and, unfortunately, is not uncommon now—for those entering the clergy to have little or no personal faith, but rather to see the position as a means to an end. Darwin could see himself as a country parson, able to carry on natural-history studies in his spare time, in the same manner as many clergymen before and since.

His change of career to clergyman required a move to one of the main English universities, so Robert Darwin arranged for his son to start his

Charles Darwin as a young man by G Richmond

studies for a theology degree at the University of Cambridge. He could not start there in October 1827, when he was accepted, as he needed to catch up on a number of studies—most notably, his knowledge of Greek. After a couple of months of work with a private tutor, Darwin began his studies at Cambridge in December 1827.

Darwin's three years there were of mixed value to him. Of those years, he said, 'my time was wasted, as far as academical studies were concerned, as completely as at Edinburgh and at school.'[4] Nevertheless, he enjoyed the atmosphere, being able to meet up with other sons of gentlemen, including not a few old acquaintances from school days. He still did not care for the classics, attending very few of the lectures. He also tried to get to grips with mathematics. During the summer of 1828, he went briefly to Barmouth, North-West Wales, taking a maths tutor with him, in the hope that he would better understand the subject—but to no avail. He preferred to spend time with his friends, reading, fishing and collecting beetles.

The one area of compulsory study that did interest him, however, was the study of the works of William Paley. He was impressed by the logic of Paley's books *Evidences of Christianity* and *Moral Philosophy*. He was particularly interested in Paley's *Natural Theology*, a book which looks to nature to find evidences for God's creative powers. *Natural Theology* is basically a prototype of a textbook for Intelligent Design! Darwin's fascination for, and love of, this book is ironic, considering that it was his own later work which caused the demise in acceptance of Paley's biological ideas. Today, there has been a resurgence of interest in Paley's ideas, many of which still have as much logical power today as they seemed to have for the young Darwin then.

Paley considered that there was actual design in nature that gave evidence for the existence of God. The most famous argument used in his *Natural Theology* is that of the watchmaker. His book begins thus:

In crossing a heath, suppose I pitched my foot against a stone, and were asked how the stone came to be there, I might possibly answer, that for any thing I knew to the contrary it had laid there for ever; nor would it, perhaps, be very easy to show the absurdity of this answer. But suppose I had found a watch, upon the ground, and it should be inquired how the watch happened to be in that place, I should hardly think of

Watch mechanism

the answer which I had before given, that for any thing I knew the watch might have always been there.[5]

Paley went on to describe the mechanism of the watch in detail, and concluded, 'There must have existed, at some time and at some place or other, an artificer or artificers who formed it for the purpose which we find it actually to answer, who comprehended its construction and designed its use.'[6] His conclusion was that the obvious elements of design in the watch implied a designer. This is the classic argument used today by the Intelligent Design movement. Remember that Paley was writing before the discoveries of DNA and the intricacy of living cells; nevertheless, he applied the design argument to nature and found it equally valid.[7] Darwin stated, 'I do not think I hardly ever admired a book more than Paley's *Natural Theology*. I could almost formerly have said it by heart.'[8]

HMS *Beagle* by Conrad Martens

Despite this interest, Darwin continued to make a poor student. He was far more interested in collecting beetles or having dinner with friends than with studying. Nevertheless, he obtained his degree in theology in 1831. It was fully his intention, at this time, to become a country clergyman, able to spend free time involved in studying natural history.

HMS *Beagle*

Darwin's intentions were not to work out, however. On 29 August 1831, he returned home to Shrewsbury from a trip to North Wales to find letters awaiting him that invited him to join the second voyage of HMS *Beagle* as it undertook a two-year survey of South America. He was to be the naturalist. This job was traditionally the preserve of the ship's surgeon, which probably explains a certain friction between Darwin and the surgeon, Robert McCormick, who was himself no mean explorer. HMS *Beagle* was to be captained by twenty-six-year-old Robert FitzRoy. FitzRoy must have felt that it would be problematic, as so young a commander, to be close to any crew member on the voyage, so it was felt appropriate that he should have a 'gentleman companion'. Twenty-two-year-old Darwin eagerly accepted the role, but his father was against the idea, seeing this as yet another opportunity for Charles to waste his time instead of pursuing a worthwhile vocation. Charles had an ally in his maternal uncle, however, who persuaded Robert Darwin that the voyage was likely to be of benefit to Charles. Robert Darwin relented, and Charles was able to take an interview with FitzRoy, whose favoured choice had just become unavailable. So, after several delays, Darwin, FitzRoy and the crew of the *Beagle* set sail from Plymouth on 27 December 1831 for what must be one of the most famous scientific voyages of all time.

A book of this brevity cannot hope to cover every detail of this famous voyage; that would take a book in its own right. Nevertheless, it is worth making some appropriate observations.

FitzRoy and Darwin were very different people. FitzRoy came from a Tory family, whereas the Darwins and the Wedgwoods were Whigs (the Tories and the Whigs were the two predominant political parties of the era). FitzRoy was also a Bible-believing Christian. He read aloud from the Bible every day, leading on-ship times of devotion. During the years of the *Beagle*'s voyage, Darwin must surely have heard the gospel. However, as we have seen, Darwin's background, though religious, was not really Christian. These differences could have led to considerable friction—indeed, on occasion there was friction—but, for the most part, the two young men got on rather well.

The prevailing geological view of the time was that of catastrophism. Catastrophists did not necessarily hold to the view that most of the world's sedimentary rock was laid down in the Flood. Many of them believed in old ages for the earth, and that there had been several catastrophes. Nevertheless, Darwin was persuaded otherwise. On the voyage, he had with him a copy of Volume 1 of *Principles of Geology* by Charles Lyell. Lyell set about popularizing a uniformitarian view in line with the earlier opinions of James Hutton. From his private correspondence, we know that Charles Lyell had a religious agenda in developing old-earth uniformitarian models for the geological processes of the past. Jonathan Henry comments,

Lyell was by training a lawyer, or in the terminology of the time, a barrister, a fact formally acknowledged in the title of the memorial volumes published after his death. Lyell's real 'hidden agenda' was revealed in private correspondence with colleagues and friends. He wrote that he had 'driven' the biblical Flood 'out of the Mosaic record'. He also revealed his plan for undermining the Bible. He would not make a frontal attack against the Scripture, but 'conceived the idea ... that if ever the Mosaic chronology could be set down [discredited] without giving offence, it would be in an historical sketch ...' Lyell's reference to 'an historical sketch' meant a work about 'historical geology' written from an evolutionary viewpoint. His well-known *Principles of Geology* was the fulfilment of this plan.

In sum, Lyell using his legal skills would manufacture an opus presenting the alleged evolutionary version of the earth's geological past. He would lead his readers to doubt the chronology of Moses and the Bible as a whole without directly attacking it and without even naming it. With his *Principles of Geology*, published when he was only in his early thirties, he succeeded no doubt beyond his wildest dreams.[9]

Darwin received Volume 2 of Lyell's three-volume work when the *Beagle* reached South America. Therefore, by the time Darwin reached the Galápagos Islands, he was thoroughly conversant with Lyell's long-age uniformitarian ideas. In proposing the evolution of species, Darwin's use of long-age principles was not formulated as a result of his famous observations of finches and tortoises; rather, he already held the long-age views before he made these observations.

It needs to be said that Darwin was a careful collector and observer. The information that he garnered on the voyage was invaluable. Creationists do not criticize his scientific methodology, merely his conclusions and the hypothesis that he developed in an attempt to explain his observations according to his uniformitarian presuppositions.

After the *Beagle*

The *Beagle* returned to Britain on 2 October 1836. Following the voyage, FitzRoy helped to produce a four-volume set of notes of this voyage and the first *Beagle* voyage. He included his own observations. The third volume of the set was written by Charles Darwin and became the first edition of

Darwin's account of the voyage. These volumes were published in 1839. During the voyage, Darwin and FitzRoy had more or less shared their opinions of Lyellian uniformitarianism, but also of an opposition to the concept of transmutation (the alteration of one species into another) of the species. Following the voyage, both men's ideas changed. Darwin produced a second version of his diary notes in 1845 in which he added his ideas about transmutation. He did not make it clear that these thoughts had developed subsequent to the voyage, rather than being formulated during it. FitzRoy, on the other hand, returned to a more Christian and biblical opinion, stating his belief once more in a literal reading of the Bible.[10]

Later, when Darwin published his *On the Origin of Species*, FitzRoy clearly felt betrayed. He attended the famous debate in 1860, in which Bishop Samuel Wilberforce attacked the concept of evolution. His contribution to the debate was not well received and he was shouted down, as he stated that *On the Origin of Species* had caused him the most acute pain.

The voyage on the *Beagle* completely changed Darwin's life. He very quickly became a scientific celebrity. Within a month of his return, he had met Charles Lyell and was soon being introduced to scientific society in London. In December of that year, Darwin moved to Cambridge in order to start the work of cataloguing his discoveries, but in March 1837 he moved to London because he was so much in demand to read papers at scientific societies. He was no longer the failed student son of a provincial physician; he was now a man of influence in scientific society.

Notes

1 **Francis Darwin,** (ed.), *The Life and Letters of Charles Darwin*, vol. 1 (London: John Murray, 1887), p. 45.

2 **Charles R. Darwin,** *The Autobiography of Charles Darwin, 1809–1882* (London: Collins, 1958), p. 57.

3 Ibid.

4 **Francis Darwin,** (ed.), *Charles Darwin: His Life Told in an Autobiographical Chapter, and in a Selected Series of his Published Letters* (London: John Murray, 1892), p. 17.

Chapter 3

5 **William Paley,** *Natural Theology* (1802; Landisville, PA: Coachwhip Publications, 2005), p. 7.

6 Ibid. p. 8.

7 Paley's design argument is criticized today by evolutionists—most notably, by **Richard Dawkins** in *The Blind Watchmaker.*

8 **Charles Darwin,** *Life and Letters of Charles Darwin*, vol. 1 (New York: D. Appleton and Co., 1911), p. 15.

9 **Jonathan F. Henry,** 'An Old Age for the Earth is the Heart of Evolution', *Creation Research Society Quarterly*, 40 /3 (2003), pp. 164–172.

10 **Robert FitzRoy,** *Narrative of the Surveying Voyages of His Majesty's Ships* Adventure *and* Beagle *Between the Years 1826 and 1836* (London: Henry Colburn, 1839), ch. 28.

The evolution of the Theory of Evolution

For since the creation of the world His invisible attributes are clearly seen, being understood by the things that are made, even His eternal power and Godhead, so that they are without excuse, because, although they knew God, they did not glorify Him as God, nor were thankful, but became futile in their thoughts, and their foolish hearts were darkened. Professing to be wise, they became fools, and changed the glory of the incorruptible God into an image made like corruptible man—and birds and four-footed animals and creeping things. (Rom. 1:20–23)

Throughout much of his life, Darwin was not a well man. He frequently suffered from problems with his heart and stomach. In addition, he gave himself a considerable amount of work—in 1837 he was writing up his journal from the voyage as well as working on a proposed book on South American geology in support of Lyell's ideas. He was also, for a while, secretary of the Geological Society. Although freed to do this work by a generous allowance from his father, Charles Darwin nevertheless did not enjoy good health. There were a number of occasions when he needed to take a break from his activities, during which he spent time in Scotland, at the family home in Shrewsbury or visiting other family members.

It was at this time that he met his cousin, Emma Wedgwood, who was to become his wife. It will be remembered that Darwin shared his father's lack of faith. Robert Darwin therefore advised Charles not to tell Emma about his doubts about religion. The younger Darwin did not follow this advice, however. This was likely to have been a source of concern to Emma throughout their lives together. The Wedgwoods were mainly Unitarians, although Emma was an Anglican. Their faith was therefore not biblical or evangelical, but was certainly not agnostic, like Darwin's. Nevertheless, Charles and Emma were married on 29 January 1839 and went to live in London.

Darwin's scientific ideas were beginning to lead him into a sort of double life. It was clear that many of his ideas on transmutation were at odds with the views of other scientists and establishment figures. He therefore tended to keep quiet about his work on evolution. The problem was that he did not as yet have an effective model of how evolution might have happened. This would take nearly two years of writing and prevarication, as well as much urging from his circle of friends and contacts, with whom he shared his ideas.

Down House

In July 1842, Darwin bought his young family a house in the village of Downe in the Kent countryside (it is now within the London Borough of Bromley). Charles, Emma and their two little children moved into the house on 14 September. On 23 September, their third child, Mary, was

Down House, Kent

born, but the baby died just three weeks later. Such family tragedies were difficult for Charles Darwin and seem to have contributed to his bouts of illness. The Darwins had ten children in total, but three, including Mary, died in childhood.

Today, Down House is in the care of English Heritage and is well worth a visit. It is preserved more or less as it was in Darwin's time. Inside the house, you can see the drawing room and study downstairs, while the upstairs rooms house some interesting exhibitions. Outside, the gardens can be enjoyed much as the Darwins would have enjoyed them, including the outbuildings: a greenhouse and Darwin's laboratory. In Darwin's day, the grounds also included a meadow and the famous Sandwalk, along which Darwin used to stroll and think as he developed his ideas.

These Down House years were long years. If the voyage on the *Beagle* had impressed Darwin so much, why did it take him so long to publish his

The Sandwalk, Down House

evolutionary ideas? The first edition of his *Beagle* journals was published in 1839; *On the Origin of Species* was published in 1859: a gap of twenty years.

The standard argument is that Darwin was nervous about the reaction that his theory might cause. Twenty years still seems a long time to wait, even if that were so. However, the intelligentsia of the time were actually open to the concept of evolutionary theory, which, after all, had already been mooted by figures such as Jean-Baptiste Lamarck and Darwin's own grandfather, Erasmus.

An alternative view of Darwin's prevarication has surfaced from time to time, most recently in a book by Roy Davies.[1] Davies supposes that Darwin's prevarication was because he really didn't know what mechanism to propose for his evolutionary theory. Indeed, Davies suggests that Darwin was wedded to an alternative model for transmutation of species—migration theory—until only a year or two before the publication of *On the Origin of Species*. Migration theory is the idea that transmutations only occurred because of enforced migrations. A more or less final blow was delivered to Darwin's migration theory by his friend Joseph Hooker, in a letter dated August 1856.[2] Up to that date at least, he had not entertained the idea of evolution by natural selection. If Davies is correct, it throws into doubt Darwin's claim for priority in discovering his evolutionary mechanism.

Some writers have assumed that Darwin must have been doing a lot of experimentation during these years. There was a little experimentation undertaken, but even his most enthusiastic biographers have suggested that it was fairly mundane work and not directly applicable to his theory. Probably more significant to Darwin's work was the way in which he took advantage of the remarkable leap in information and communication technology that had occurred in Victorian times—the advent of an efficient and global postal service. Darwin became a prolific letter-writer, corresponding with his peers around the world. He would frequently send aspects of his ideas to other theorists to ask for their opinions, and he built up a number of professional relationships with people he hadn't actually met. In many ways, these means of communication were as significant to his work as the Internet is to many of us today.

During this time, Darwin was being strongly encouraged to publish his thoughts by Charles Lyell, who had become his friend and mentor. Lyell was clearly keen that Darwin should take the credit for publishing a more 'workable' theory of evolution than the previous offerings from people such as Lamarck or Erasmus Darwin. Darwin's fans suggest that he wanted to get his theory right; a neutral observer might suppose that his prevarication was due to not entirely knowing what he was doing. In the end, events would propel Darwin into publication.

Towards publication

One of the most significant personalities involved in leading Darwin to publish his book was Alfred Russel Wallace. Wallace was a naturalist from a very different social class from that of Darwin. Hailing from a Southern-Welsh family of modest means, he travelled the world, earning his way by collecting items for the armchair naturalists back home. He enters our story in spring 1856, when Darwin received a package from Lyell that included a paper by Wallace, outlining Wallace's ideas on the transmutation of species. Lyell was of the opinion that Wallace's paper was making similar points to Darwin's work. As he had so often done before, Lyell urged Darwin to publish his work, lest he be beaten to it. Darwin's opinion was that he was still not ready to publish. As we have seen, one suggestion as to why Darwin did not publish is that he was still not sure of a mechanism for his theory of evolution; this mechanism became clearer in 1858.

In June 1858, Darwin received a letter from Wallace with a copy of his manuscript, entitled *On the Tendency of Varieties to Depart Indefinitely from the Original Type*. The exact date of the arrival of this letter is controversial and may have a bearing on the whole history of evolutionary theory.

Darwin maintained that he received the letter on 18 June 1858. He was horrified. Wallace's ideas were almost identical to his own. Indeed, in an article written to commemorate the 100th anniversary of the publication of *On the Origin of Species*, one commentator said, 'It was Darwin's unpublished conception down to the last detail, independently duplicated by a man sitting in a hut at the world's end.'[3] At the time, Wallace was working in Ternate in the Malay Archipelago.

What happened next appears to have been an unholy rush into publication. Darwin's friends Charles Lyell and Joseph Hooker arranged for a special meeting of the Linnean Society in London. This society, founded in 1788, exists for the study and dissemination of taxonomy (the naming of species) and natural history. Wallace's paper was to be read at this meeting, along with a paper of Darwin's, which was actually hurriedly compiled from an essay written by Darwin in 1844 and a letter to the American naturalist Asa Gray in 1857. Although this was supposedly a joint presentation, neither Darwin nor Wallace was present. Darwin's baby son had only just died of scarlet fever, while Wallace was still in Ternate, his permission for the reading having been neither granted nor sought. Given the 1844 date of Darwin's incomplete work, the Linnean Society credited both men with being co-discoverers of the theory, but with Darwin having priority.

Roy Davies[4] has suggested a slightly different timeline, which makes some sense of the indecent haste. He relates that Wallace had sent a letter to a relative of his at the same time that he posted his paper to Darwin. This letter arrived on 3 June 1858. Davies supposes that Darwin must also have received his letter on 3 June and lied about receiving it on 18 June. Such a blatant lie would not be out of character with the childhood lies of Darwin related in Chapter 2. It is certainly the case that, on 10 June, Darwin had written to Hooker, showing that he had cracked the mechanism problem. If the traditional timescale is correct, Darwin's letter to Hooker was written eight days before the bombshell of reading Wallace's work. If Davies' timescale is correct, Darwin wrote to Hooker seven days *after* reading Wallace's ideas, which would surely make Darwin guilty of plagiarism. Whatever the order of events, who knows how long Darwin would have prevaricated before publication if Wallace had not been on the ball? Either way, just over a year later, Darwin's *magnum opus, On the Origin of Species* (full title: *On the Origin of Species by Means of Natural Selection; or, the Preservation of Favoured Races in the Struggle for Life*), was published. It has to be said that, during his lifetime, there was no suggestion from Wallace that he disagreed with the official account of the events leading to the publication of Darwin's theory. It must also be mentioned in this context that Wallace was a spiritualist and he was sure that his theory came from his spirit guides. Could it be that Satan's evolutionary ideas, as mentioned in Chapter 1, came to fruition first through a spiritualist in a feverish tropical trance, then through the more acceptable pen of an establishment gentleman?

Family and faith

One enduring image of Darwin is as a family man. It is certainly true that the Darwins had a large family—they had ten children in all.

The deaths of three of Darwin's children affected him deeply. Some have seen in this the reason for his rejection of faith—especially the death of his favourite daughter, Annie, in 1851. While not doubting the depth of Darwin's emotions over this and other tragedies, we have noted that there was never really any faith in Darwin's head or heart. It is likely that Annie's death merely confirmed him in his opinion on the non-existence of God.

Human evolution and other matters

In his *On the Origin of Species*, Darwin had fought shy of suggesting that human beings had evolved. Yet we can see an evolutionary—and, indeed, pseudo-racist—view of other people groups in some of his other writings. For example, in 1845, he made this observation concerning the Fuegian people that he had met at Tierra del Fuego: 'I could not have believed how wide was the difference between savage and civilized man: it is greater than between a wild and domesticated animal, inasmuch as in man there is a greater power of improvement.'[5]

His fuller ideas on the supposed evolution of human beings came in his book *The Descent of Man* (1871). It is this book that has robbed human beings of their dignity before God and has proclaimed a 'gospel' that we are nothing more than animals ourselves, made in the image of nature rather than the image of God. As Darwin himself put it, 'Man still bears in his bodily frame the indelible stamp of his lowly origin.'[6]

Darwin's ideas were of their time. Contrary to popular opinion today, the idea of evolution was not so outrageous, particularly to the society of the intelligentsia. For a society which was overthrowing the authority of the Bible in a number of areas, Darwinism was an idea whose time had come and which resonated with the opinions of the age.

Westminster Abbey, London

Darwin, never a well man, became particularly ill in late 1881, eventually dying on 19 April 1882. As a measure of how he was perceived in the nation at the time, the family's plans to have him buried in Downe village were thwarted and a petition was raised to have him buried in Westminster Abbey. It is therefore somewhat ironic that at this iconically traditional centre of British Christian culture lies the body of a man whose work has done more than that of any other to undermine that same faith and culture.

An apocryphal story, publicized by a certain Lady Hope, related that Darwin recanted of evolution on his deathbed and became a Christian. Such claims were refuted by Darwin's own children and contradicted by his wife. It is likely that there is no truth in the story. It serves only to remind us that Darwin's ideas and personality have always been controversial. Today, a new generation need to assess his ideas for themselves, and should look with open eyes at the damage those ideas have caused.

Notes

1 **Roy Davies,** *The Darwin Conspiracy* (London: Golden Square Books, 2008).

2 Ibid. p. 76.

3 **L. Eiseley,** 'Alfred Russel Wallace', *Scientific American*, 200/2 (1959), p. 80.

4 **Davies,** *The Darwin Conspiracy.*

5 **Charles Darwin,** *A Naturalist's Voyage round the World: Journal of Researches into the Natural History and Geology of the Countries Visited During the Voyage of HMS* Beagle *under the Command of Captain FitzRoy, RN* (1845; 1928, London: John Murray), pp. 205–231.

6 **Charles Darwin,** *The Descent of Man* (London: John Murray, 1871), p. 405.

Darwin's worldview

In the beginning was the Word, and the Word was with God, and the Word was God. He was in the beginning with God. All things were made through Him, and without Him nothing was made that was made. (John 1:1–3)

For by him all things were created that are in heaven and that are on earth, visible and invisible ... All things were created through him and for him. (Col. 1:16)

The 1859 publication of *On the Origin of Species* has affected the worldview of every generation since, encouraging people to think that they are the products of chance random processes and that they ultimately have no reason for existence. The book has had an incredible effect on Western society and has never been out of print since the first edition of 1,250 copies was sold out the first day. Darwin knew that his work had a profound influence on the scientific world and he was happy to boast of this: 'with such moderate abilities as I possess, it is truly surprising that thus I should have influenced to a considerable extent the beliefs of scientific men on some important points.'[1]

Why was *On the Origin of Species* so popular? There can be no reason other than that the UK public were ready to embrace an alternative to the biblical creation account. The new spirit of the age was one of unbelief, even though there were religious revivals in Scotland and Ireland around that time. Darwin's book got mixed reviews and experts of his day were by no means agreed on its correctness, yet within a decade, evolution became the accepted orthodoxy. Through Archbishop Frederick Temple, the Church of England had no answer to this agnosticism except to claim, 'The doctrine of evolution leaves the argument for an intelligent Creator and Governor of the earth stronger than before'![2]

Charles Darwin at 51

Chapter 5

Darwin's studies

As we have seen, after leaving the University of Edinburgh without a degree, Darwin studied divinity at Cambridge but never took a living as a cleric, for he was more interested in biology than theology. He wrote several books in his chosen field of study, such as *Various Contrivances by which British and Foreign Orchids are Fertilised by Insects* (1862), *The Effects of Cross and Self Fertilisation in the Vegetable Kingdom* (1876) and *The Formation of Vegetable Mould Through the Action of Worms* (1881). Sadly (and as we have also already seen), his faith was not evangelical, so his developing liberal views on the Bible, often expressed during his trip on the *Beagle*, were a constant irritation to Captain Robert FitzRoy. This five-year voyage of discovery changed his life and the publication of *On the Origin of Species* was to set modern agnosticism on a long road of opposition to the Bible with a zeal and a false assurance it never possessed before.

We have seen that Darwin did not invent the theory of evolution; this dubious honour belongs to others. Darwin said that two books influenced him more than any others: Alexander von Humboldt's *Personal Narrative* and J. F. Herschel's *Preliminary Discourse on the Study of Natural Philosophy*; 'they stirred me up to a burning zeal.' The anonymously written *Vestiges of the Natural History of Creation*, plus the impending draft paper by Alfred Russel Wallace that outlined a theory of natural selection very similar to Darwin's own, pushed him to publish. It was, however, German monk and abbot George Mendel's ideas on natural selection that saved Darwinism from rejection. Despite all this, the theory of evolution has been attributed to Charles Darwin in the popular mind and his book *The Descent of Man* (1871), in which he made clear his belief that man is descended from the apes, established his literary immortality. His reason for writing it is given in his autobiography:

Although in *On the Origin of Species*, the derivation of any particular species is never discussed, yet I thought it best, in order that no honourable man should accuse me of concealing my views, to add that by the work in question 'light would be thrown on the origin of man and his history'. It would have been useless and injurious to the success of the book to have paraded without giving any evidence of my conviction with respect to his origin.

From Darwin's autobiography we see the history of his path from Unitarianism to agnosticism, when he clearly states that the voyage on the *Beagle* was by far the most important event in his life and determined his whole career. Sadly, however, his testimony contains the record of his spiritual decline. He begins the story of his descent into agnosticism by admitting,

Whilst on board the *Beagle* I was quite orthodox, and I remember being heartily laughed at by several of the officers (though themselves orthodox) for quoting the Bible as an unanswerable authority on some point of morality. I suppose it was the novelty of the argument that amused them. But I had gradually come, by this time, to see that the Old Testament from its manifestly false history of the world, with the Tower of Babel, the rainbow as a sign, etc., etc., and from its attributing to God the feelings of a revengeful tyrant, was no more to be trusted than the sacred books of the Hindoos, or the beliefs of any barbarian. I gradually came to disbelieve in Christianity as a divine revelation. The fact that many false religions have spread over large portions of the earth like wild-fire had some weight with me. Beautiful as is the morality of the New Testament, it can hardly be denied that its perfection depends in part on the interpretation which we now put on metaphors and allegories ... But I was very unwilling to give up my belief ... I found it more and more difficult, with free scope given to my imagination, to invent evidence which would suffice to convince me. Thus disbelief crept over me at a very slow rate, but was at last complete.

With his admission that unbelief filled his heart, it is clear that Darwin's conscience became so closed to the light of the Scriptures that he arrogantly said that the rate of unbelief, although slow, gave him 'no distress' and he admitted never doubting again, even for a single second, that his conclusion to reject Christianity as untrue was correct. He said, 'I can indeed hardly see how anyone ought to wish Christianity to be true.' Thus for the rest of his life, Darwin rejected belief in miracles, doubted the veracity of the Gospels and decidedly rejected the doctrine of eternal punishment.

What did Darwin believe?

There are two strands to Darwinism. The first is that all life evolved over long time periods from a single prototype cell. The other is the notion of natural selection, which assumes that beneficial changes (mutations) happen in creatures very suddenly and that these become permanent features in a species or kind, being passed on to the next generation. Darwin, however, did not invent the term 'survival of the fittest'; this was coined five years after his *On the Origin of Species* was published and was used by Herbert Spencer in his 1864 book, *Principles of Biology*. Darwin defined evolution as descent with modification. This, however, as author Bill Bryson has noted, was quickly seen to be flawed by Fleeming Jenkin, a Scottish engineer, who pointed out that a mutation in one bird would not be passed on as it would be diluted in the process of reproduction, diluted again in the next generation, and so on.[3]

Darwin's worldview found him rejecting the argument of design that he had previously accepted; he wrote, 'The old argument of design in nature, as given by Dr Paley, which formerly seemed to me so conclusive, fails, now that the law of natural selection has been discovered.'[4] He reckoned that 'There seems to be no more design in the variability of organic beings and in the action of natural selection, than in the course which the wind blows'. But later on in his testimony, he seems to contradict himself when he states, 'Some other considerations, moreover, lead to the belief that all sentient beings have been formed so as to enjoy, as a general rule, happiness.' He seems here to allow for a design and plan whose end is to bring creatures to a place of happiness. This, of course, is what the Bible teaches; an intelligent, almighty Creator made man in his image and sent his only Son to save the world in order to bestow joy and peace upon the souls of fallen sinners (John 3:16; 2 Cor. 5:19).

Any experience of Christianity Darwin had in his soul was short-lived; he said, 'Formerly I was led by feelings … to the firm conviction of the existence of God, and of the immortality of the soul.' Sadly, he reveals the darkness that came over his soul after he was caught up in evolutionary ideas: 'but now … I am like a man who has become colour-blind … Therefore I cannot see that such inward convictions and feelings are of any weight as evidence of what really exists.' Nothing more clearly shows the deadly spiritual influence of evolution than this spiritual decline in the life and soul of Charles Darwin when he embraced as true his own scientific analysis that contradicted the Bible's account of origins. However, he seemed to remain a theist of sorts:

Another source of conviction in the existence of God, connected with the reason and not with the feelings, impresses me as having much more weight. This follows from the extreme difficulty or rather impossibility of conceiving this immense and wonderful universe, including man with his capacity of looking far backwards and far into futurity, as the result of blind chance or necessity. When thus reflecting I feel compelled to look to a First Cause having an intelligent mind in some degree analogous to that of man; and I deserve to be called a Theist.

It appears that he was unsure of what to believe when he wrote *On the Origin of Species*, but he slipped slowly and permanently into agnosticism thereafter.

THE DARWINIAN VIEW OF THE ORIGIN OF MAN
MUTATIONS + NATURAL SELECTION + RANDOM CHANGE = EVOLUTION OVER
BILLIONS OF YEARS

Darwin's children
Thus we see that Charles Darwin appears to have struggled with the emptiness of atheism. However, many of his followers in the 20th and 21st centuries have rejected theism and Christianity. Oxford naturalist, evolutionary biologist, author and Professor for the Public Understanding of Science at Oxford University, Richard Dawkins, who is proud to be called a Darwinian, believes that the universe has 'no design, no purpose, no evil and no good, nothing but blind pitiless indifference'.[5] For modern Darwinians there is a foundational assumption that there is no God. To them, Christianity seems to be utterly irrational. Dawkins likens it to believing in a teapot orbiting the sun.[6] But is it not true that millions of teapots *are* orbiting the sun as they sit in kitchens and on tables in homes and restaurants on planet Earth as it makes its way through space at 108,000 km an hour?

However, Dawkins is not qualified to speak with authority on questions

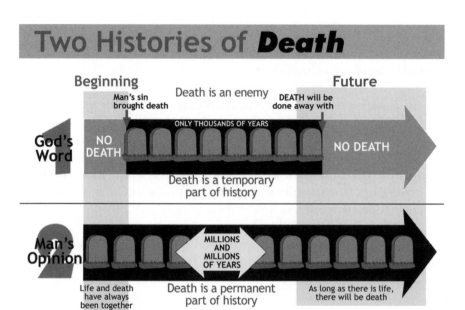

Two Histories of *Death*

Beginning   Death is an enemy   **Future**

Man's sin brought death

DEATH will be done away with

God's Word

ONLY THOUSANDS OF YEARS

NO DEATH

NO DEATH

Death is a temporary part of history

Man's Opinion

MILLIONS AND MILLIONS OF YEARS

Life and death have always been together

Death is a permanent part of history

As long as there is life, there will be death

Beginning   **Future**

© 2006 *Answers in Genesis*

of theology because he is a scientist who has no degrees in this field of study. This objection might seem out of turn but for the fact that Dawkins is so insistent that only scientists are capable of understanding the universe. I am not alone in thinking that he is an ignoramus when it comes to theology. Terry Eagleton, in a review of Dawkins' *God Delusion*, points out, 'Imagine someone holding forth on Biology whose only knowledge of the subject is the *Book of British Birds*, and you have a rough idea of what it feels like to read Richard Dawkins on Theology.'[7] In his book *The Dawkins Letters*, David Robertson makes the same point. Addressing Dawkins directly, he says, 'Your understanding of Christian Theology is shockingly bad', and 'I am astonished at how out of touch you are with modern biblical scholarship'.[8] Dawkins has a similar attitude himself towards his opponents and will not share a platform with a young-earth creationist. Why? 'I don't like giving them the oxygen of respectability, the feeling that if they're up on a platform debating with a scientist, there must be real disagreement. One side of the debate is wholly ignorant. It is as though you knew nothing of physics and were passionately arguing against Einstein's theory of relativity,' he says.[9]

Yet Christians believe that it is important that we bring every thought to the obedience of Christ and to submission to his sovereign and over-arching Word. J. M. Frame, in his book *Apologetics to the Glory of God*, insists that there are distinctive Christian views on history, science, psychology, business, economics, labour, sociology, education, and so on. The four most important things to remember about the Christian worldview, he claims, are: first, the absolute personality of God; second, the distinction between Creator and creature; third, the sovereignty of God; and fourth, the Trinity. Contrasted with this is the worldview of the sinner that is 'twisted and unreliable'. 'Rationalistic philosophy declares human reason to be the final standard. Scepticism says that truth is unattainable.'[10] Creation of man on the sixth day (Gen. 1:26–31) is regarded as a myth by both naturalism, the ruling philosophy of modern culture, and rationalism, which asserts that knowledge is to be put together primarily on the basis of the self-evident beliefs of human reason. Dawkins claims that naturalism, empowered by Darwin's theory, can explain everything. This, he believes, has 'made it possible to be an intellectually fulfilled atheist'.[11]

Darwinian dilemma

The challenge of improbability which natural selection brings to the origins debate is a real problem for evolutionists. Their assertion that evolution is a chance happening through random processes is highly improbable indeed. This improbability is, however, dismissed by Dawkins, who says, 'Natural selection is a cumulative process, which breaks the problem of improbability up into small pieces.' He reckons that each stage in the evolutionary ladder is achievable by lesser steps and claims that creationists do not 'understand the power of *accumulation*' (his italics).[12] But this *is* what creationists mean when they state that the probability of life originating by chance random processes is so small that it is statistically improbable. It is not only creationists who say this; Sir Fred Hoyle, the famous British mathematician and astronomer, said that

The tree of life

'the statistical improbabilities of a single cell originating by random processes (in the primitive atmosphere of the assumed 4.6 billion years of earth's history) was one chance in 10 raised to the power 4000'![13] Dawkins himself quotes with dismissive disdain Fred Hoyle's statement that 'The probability of life originating on earth is no greater than the chance that a hurricane, sweeping through a scrapyard, would have the luck to assemble a Boeing 747'.[14]

Other evolutionists see this point more clearly than Dawkins. Bill Bryson, for example, in his book *A Short History of Nearly Everything*, constantly states that the existence of *Homo sapiens* on earth is due to numerous chance happenings, otherwise mankind just would not be here today; however, he also says that each process of micro-evolution (very small changes) was so improbable that if it had not happened, the next stage in the evolutionary tree could not have proceeded and human life as we know it today would not exist. Speaking about the formation of the earth and its primordial atmosphere of toxic gases, Bryson has written, 'Hardly the sort of stuff we would associate with life, and yet from this noxious stew life formed ... had we not had the benefit of a greenhouse effect, the Earth might well have frozen over permanently, and life might never have got a foothold. But somehow it did.'[15] In other words, the statistical improbabilities are so exceedingly large in *all* stages for them to be utterly impossible. However, because of Bryson's evolutionary bias, he assumes that the impossible must have happened, otherwise we would not be here at all! He takes no account of God, nor is God in his thoughts. This, of course, is why evolutionists hypothesize about billions of years. For evolution to work, very large amounts of time are required. This is the only answer they can come up with that appears to solve the improbability. If they did not have lots and lots and lots of time, their precious theory would not seem, on the surface, to work. R. Laird Harris's comment is relevant here:

The evolutionary view, from almost any angle, requires long periods of time. But long periods of time do not require evolution. There is a remarkable recent discovery of the coelacanth fish off the eastern coast of Africa which has not evolved but is evidently exactly like its fossil remains of allegedly 400 million years ago. Evolution demands time but time does not automatically cause evolution. God has plenty of time. He is eternal.[16]

Paul Davies, who has estimated that, over ten billion years, the odds of random permutations of molecules assembling just one molecule of DNA is much less than 1 out of 10 to the power 30,000 (i.e. 10 followed by 30,000 zeros), says, 'How can an incredibly complex organism, so harmoniously organized into an integrated functioning unit, perhaps endowed with exceedingly intricate and efficient organs such as eyes and ears, be the product of a series of pure accidents?'[17]

Darwinian denial

Evolutionists like Richard Dawkins label those who accept the Bible's account of creation in six days as 'fundamentalists', a title Dawkins loves to throw about in an unhelpful way. He, however, reveals that *his* faith is not in the Word of God but in fallible men who can make mistakes; he says, 'I, as a scientist believe ... not because of reading a holy book but because I have believed the evidence ... when a science book is wrong, somebody eventually discovers the mistake and it is corrected in subsequent books.'[18] He admits that scientists can get things wrong because there are many things that science does not know; no matter how much scientists do know, there is an infinite amount they do not know. We believe that this possibility of error is true of the evolutionary hypothesis called Darwinism. Dawkins suggests wrongly that Christians love to challenge science because they are blind to scientific discovery and are set against experimental and observable (empirical) scientific work, but he is mistaken. Creationists make a clear distinction between empirical and doctrinaire/ideological science. The former is generally received well, while the latter is regarded as speculation because it is atheistic in its presuppositions and beliefs. Creationists and evolutionists have the same evidence—biological, geological, chemical and so on—but they interpret it differently according to their worldviews. Darwinian evolutionists like Dawkins are not unprejudiced, unbiased or impartial, even though they might like to think they are. It is obvious that they cannot tolerate the Christian mindset or allow for errors in their own philosophy. They are convinced that it is Christians who are seriously flawed because Darwinism—the ascent of species through time (phylogeny)—is their perceived truth and saviour. Dawkins is so biased that he rejects the historicity of the New Testament and its eyewitness accounts from those who knew Jesus Christ or who researched his life before writing about it shortly after his death (Luke 1:1–4; John 1:14–18; 2 Peter 1:16–21; 1 John 1:1–4; Gal. 1:18–24). His rejection is irrational.

Modern Darwinians conjure up all sorts of theories when speculating about the origin of belief in a creator God. They have worked hard to come up with a definitive answer to the source of humankind's persistent and innate yearning for fellowship with their Maker, but without success.[19] But the question remains: Is there a God, and, if so, what is he like? Christians know that the Bible never questions the existence of an almighty, eternal creator God of the universe and that his self-revelation is found in the sixty-six books of Holy Scripture.

What is God like? We cannot answer these questions adequately without referring to his self-revelation in history as recorded in the Scriptures of the Old and New Testaments. They tell us *what* and *who* God is and they reveal his attributes. It is important that, when we think on the nature and personality of God, we ask the question 'What is God?' for this will help us to grasp his greatness. In the words of the Shorter Catechism:

Q4: What is God?

A: God is a spirit, infinite, eternal, and unchangeable, in his being, wisdom, power, holiness, justice, goodness and truth.

Darwinism wants to make the Christian religion subject to evolutionary development when it argues that the history of religion has moved (evolved) through various stages from polytheism (believing in many gods) through monotheism (believing in one God) to atheism. However, as McGrath says, 'The evidence simply isn't there to allow us to speak about any kind of "natural progression" from polytheism to monotheism—and hence to atheism.'[20]

Chapter 5

Notes

1 **Charles Darwin,** *The Autobiography of Charles Darwin, 1809–1882* (London: Collins, 1958), p. 145. I am grateful to this book for all other quotes from Darwin in this chapter.

2 **Colin Brown,** *Philosophy and the Christian Faith* (London: Tyndale Press, 1971), p. 150.

3 **Bill Bryson,** *A Short History of Nearly Everything* (London: Transworld, 2004), p. 473.

4 As we have seen, Darwin read **Dr Paley's** *Evidences of Christianity* while he studied Divinity at Cambridge.

5 Quoted in **Alister McGrath,** *The Dawkins Delusion* (London: SPCK, 2007), p. 30. Dawkins wrote in his collection of essays *A Devil's Chaplin* (1993) that, as a scientist, he is a Darwinian.

6 **McGrath,** *The Dawkins Delusion*, p. 28.

7 Quoted in **McGrath,** *The Dawkins Delusion*, p. 4.

8 **David Robertson,** *The Dawkins Letters* (Fearn: Christian Focus, 2008), pp. 53, 60.

9 *The Times Magazine*, 22 July 2008.

10 **J. M. Frame,** *Apologetics to the Glory of God* (Phillipsburg, NJ: Presbyterian & Reformed, 1994), pp. 31–53.

11 Quoted in **John Byl,** *The Divine Challenge* (Edinburgh: Banner of Truth, 2004), p.84.

12 **Richard Dawkins,** *The God Delusion* (London: Transworld, 2007), p. 147.

13 Quoted in **Luther D. Sutherland,** *Darwin's Enigma* (Santee, CA: Master Books, 1988), p. 58.

14 **Dawkins,** *The God Delusion*, pp. 137-138.

15 **Bryson,** *A Short History*, p. 63.

16 **R. Laird Harris,** 'The Length of the Creative Days in Genesis 1', in **J. A. Pipa** and **D. W. Hall,** (eds.), *Did God Create in Six Days?* (White Hall, WV: Tolle Lege Press, 2005), p. 102.

17 Quoted in **Byl,** *The Divine Challenge*, p. 85.

18 **Richard Dawkins,** *The God Delusion* (London: Houghton Mifflin Harcourt, 2006), p. 282.

19 **McGrath,** *The Dawkins Delusion*, pp. 29–31.

20 Ibid. p. 31.

Darwinism in biblical perspective

In the day that God created man, He made him in the likeness of God. (Gen. 5:1)

And He has made from one blood every nation of men to dwell on all the face of the earth. (Acts 17:26)

The greatest difficulty for evolutionists is to explain how life began in the first place. For atheists, one explanation that originated with the Greeks and has been around for centuries is the idea of spontaneous generation. Now Darwinism has replaced that crazy notion with what it believes to be a scientifically proven evolutionary hypothesis. However, this results in the rejection of the Bible's explanation of origins.

Loud voices

Over the last 200 years, the Bible's teaching has been challenged by naturalism and rationalism, as well as by Darwinism. The philosophers David Hume (1711–1776) and Voltaire (François-Marie Arouet, 1694–1778) both criticized organized religion and its appeal to the supernatural. Others have done the same. French philosopher Jacques Derrida (1930–2004) and his postmodern philosophy, which denies objective truth, have confused thousands of university students. Richard Dawkins and his latest book, *The God Delusion*, are full of invective towards God, Christ and the Bible, in a vain attempt to kill off true religion.

The voice of Darwinism is very loud and it is heard on every continent of the globe through the media of radio, TV and satellite broadcasting. It is propelled into millions of homes through the Internet, while billions of schoolchildren and university students come daily under the sound of its propaganda in their places of learning. But God also has his voices, and they have been speaking to humankind for thousands of years. They are, firstly, the voice of natural revelation: 'The heavens declare the glory of God; and the firmament [the expanse of heaven] shows His handiwork' (Ps. 19:1). This does not, however, mean that we can ignore the Bible's account of creation in favour of science when it speaks on origins or about the age of the earth, as Ken Ham notes:

Those who promote nature as a missing aspect of God's revelation (the so-called '67th book of the Bible') need to understand two crucial fallacies with this idea: first, nature is cursed; second, our observations of nature are not independent from our presuppositions. When we examine these problems, we see that nature should never be put on the same level as the Bible.[1]

Secondly, and more importantly, the voices in the books of Scripture that together are called the Holy Bible reveal to us what has happened in the past when it comes to origins. The Bible is made up of sixty-six books written over a period of around 1,500 years and it is regarded by Christians as God's infallible Word; as one evangelical statement of faith puts it,

God has revealed Himself in the Bible, which consists of the Old and New Testaments alone. Every word was inspired by God through human authors, so that the Bible as originally given is in its entirety the Word of God, without error and fully reliable in fact and doctrine. The Bible alone speaks with final authority and is always sufficient for all matters of belief and practice.[2]

Thus it is through this objective revelation given to us by God that we learn about God and the gospel of his Son, Jesus Christ. But not only this; where Scripture speaks of origins, it is without error and fully reliable. The Bible is not only from God, it is also about God's work as Creator as well as Father.

When it comes to the origin of human beings, the Bible does not allow Darwin's notion of millions of years of change and natural selection to produce growth from a single cell to fully developed *Homo sapiens*. The Darwinian evolutionary hypothesis does not make sense alongside the Bible, which clearly states that mankind was made from the dust of the

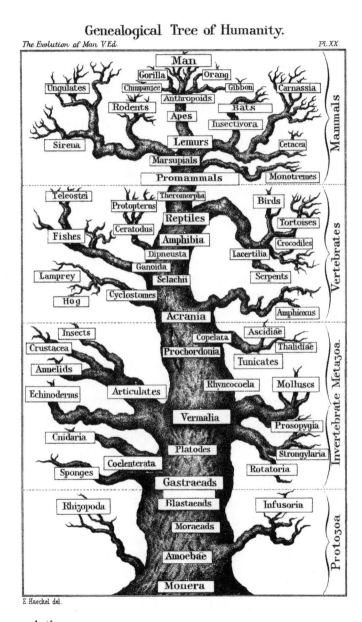

Genealogical Tree of Humanity.

Human evolution

ground (Gen. 2:7; 3:19b) and in the image of God on Day 6 of the creation week. During that sixth day, God said, 'Let Us make man in Our image, according to Our likeness' (Gen. 1:26). The words 'image' and 'likeness' are synonyms and therefore do not need distinction; as Calvin says, 'We know that it was customary with the Hebrews to repeat the same thing in different words ... the second term was added for the sake of explanation.'[3] Darwinism makes man one of the higher animals which evolved from ape-like creatures, but the Bible likens mankind to God himself, and that makes man unique. This likeness enables man to have conscious fellowship with God using the mind and affections. Because of this, men and women can call God 'Father' and talk to him in prayer (Luke 11:2). It also means that those in Christ display lives of righteousness and holiness that express the essential spiritual nature of God (Matt. 5:16; Eph. 4:24; Col. 3:10). This is best seen in Jesus Christ, as Douglas F. Kelly says: 'Christ, in the most basic sense, shows us who Adam was before the Fall: an embodied, potentially immortal spirit, graciously granted the capacity of holy and loving fellowship with his heavenly Father.'[4]

According to its kind

All life is amazingly complex and made up of cells that regulate themselves, help each other and reproduce according to their kind (Gen. 1:24). The information to build and control humans is thought to be stored in the forty-six chromosomes that are contained in a cell's nucleus. Each chromosome consists of DNA (deoxyribonucleic acid) and contains millions of molecules. The amount of information contained in each cell nucleus is extraordinary. Each chromosome can be divided into various units called genes. It has been found that the cells that make up the human body 'use very modern technology involving digital logic, analogue–digital conversion, and signal integration'.[5] In the created order there is male and female; this reveals to us that man was created first, as Genesis 1 and 2 state. Douglas Kelly explains why:

In both places [both Gen. 1 and 2] we are told that the male was created first. Genetic research confirms this, for the male has both X chromosomes (which engender females) and Y chromosomes (which engender males), whereas the female has only X chromosomes. If the female had been created first, and the male taken out of her body, then reproduction would have been impossible, for there would have been nothing but X chromosomes, in which case only females could have been reproduced. Instead the male has the genetic material so that the female could be taken out of him, and be genetically related to him 'in the same kind' and then through relationship to her be able to procreate male and female.[6]

DNA, although an amazing entity, is a dead and inert molecule, so how did life begin? Douglass Hofstradter comments, 'There are various theories of life. They all run around on this most central of central questions: "how did the Genetic Code, along with the mechanisms for its translation, originate"? For the moment, we shall have to content ourselves with a sense of wonder and awe, rather than with an answer.'[7] Three thousand years ago, Israel's King David possessed this wonder and awe, and today, honest men and women still acknowledge the wonder of it all.

When David thought on the amazing physical design of man, with man's superior intellectual and spiritual abilities, he wrote, 'I will praise You, for I am fearfully and wonderfully made; marvelous are Your works' (Ps. 139:14). King David had not seen an X-ray of the human body, nor was he a student of anatomy, biology or genetics, yet he believed that the human body was intelligently made and wonderfully adapted to live on earth. His reaction was to give God the glory for the wonderful design, complexity and beauty of the human frame. He reacted with holy awe at the sophistication and splendour of man made in God's image. Man is weak, yet strong; subject to death, but heir of eternal life; born untaught, yet possessing an innate knowledge of the eternal God. When David wrote the words of Psalm 8, was he thinking about the design and abilities of human organs such as the eyes, heart, mind and skin, or perhaps about human achievements in language, music and writing? If so, it would explain why he was full of the praise of the Almighty:

When I consider Your heavens, the work of Your fingers,
The moon and the stars, which You have ordained,
What is man that You are mindful of him,

And the son of man that You visit him?
For You have made him a little lower than the angels,
And You have crowned him with glory and honor.
You made him to have dominion over the works of Your hands;
You have put all things under his feet,
All sheep and oxen—
Even the beasts of the field,
The birds of the air,
And the fish of the sea
That pass through the paths of the sea.
O Lord, our Lord,
How excellent is Your name in all the earth!
(Ps. 8:3–9)

We see from these verses that the Bible teaches that God made Planet Earth for Adam and his posterity to look after: 'You made him to have dominion over the works of Your hands; You have put all things under his feet …' This is the cultural mandate given to Adam and Eve in the Garden: 'Be fruitful and multiply; fill the earth and subdue it; have dominion over the fish of the sea, over the birds of the air, and over every living thing that moves on the earth' (Gen. 1:28)—and it is still in force today. Mankind must ensure that the rule it exercises on the planet is balanced, wise and works to conserve its natural resources. Not only so, but there must be humane care of the lesser creatures to enable the planet to retain, sustain and maintain life for years to come. John Currid says, 'Only humans have been endowed with the status of royalty in and over the created order': 'You have made him a little lower than the angels, and You have crowned him with glory and honor' (Ps. 8:5).[8]

Was Adam real?

The Bible fixes the origin of the human race in the Garden of Eden (Gen. 1–2). This is contrary to the Darwinian idea of long ages and chance random processes. Ape-men and hunter–gatherers are not to be found in the Scriptures, yet every child is taught Darwinian ideas at school. Instead, we read that, after God created Adam, he placed him in Eden to 'tend and keep

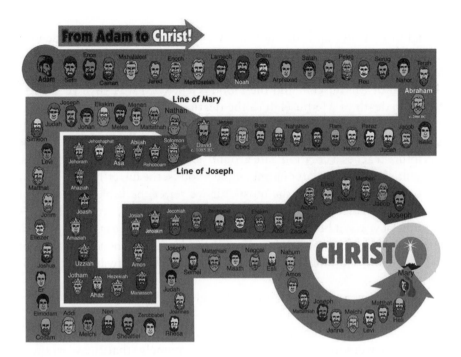

From Adam to Christ

it' (Gen. 2:15). He also told him to 'fill the earth and subdue it' (Gen. 1:28). There is no hint of Adam and Eve being ape-like creatures who had evolved over millions of years. They were to be farmers and shepherds: 'have dominion over … every living thing that moves on the earth' (Gen. 1:28).

Was Adam a real person, and was he the progenitor of the human race? Genesis 5 helps us with this question.

It opens by telling us, 'This is the book of the genealogy of Adam.' Here we have a register of names; a history which gives an account of the descent from one ancestor to another, beginning with Adam, the first man. In this chapter, the age of each person and his destiny are given (see v. 24), so we have a source of biographical history in genealogical format that yields a timeline from the creation of Adam to Christ. Professor Andy McIntosh's study of this topic has led him to write, 'The Scriptures read straightforwardly and do not allow for any gaps in the Genesis genealogies, except in one minor instance, where, at the most, a few hundred years may be inserted.' McIntosh calculates that from Adam to the death of Methuselah and the Flood (Gen. 5:27) was 1656 years, and from the death of Methuselah to the death of Abraham (Gen. 25:7) was around 467 years. This means that from Adam to Abraham was about 2,123 years. Most historians reckon Abraham to have lived c. 2000 BC, thus 'Scripture teaches a creation date around 4000 BC. Even accounting for the difficulties … and the later dating of the Exodus, the uncertainty is only of the order of 200 years at the most'.[9] If we reject the Bible's timeline of history as revealed by the genealogies and instead work with evolution's millions of years, it becomes necessary to fit millions of years and ape-men into the Bible's historical framework. This cannot be done without marginalizing the biblical evidence and rationalizing away the truth of Scripture.

God has given us *four* major genealogies in the Scriptures (Gen. 5; 1 Chr. 1–9; Matt. 1:1–17 and Luke 3:23–38) in order that we have a historical timeline from Adam to Christ and so that we get the message which they were intended to communicate, namely, that the world was created about 6,000 years ago. Archbishop James Ussher calculated that creation was around 4004 BC. He, of course, is ridiculed by Darwinians such as Christopher Hitchens, who, in his vile book *God is Not Great*, lampoons Ussher, saying, 'If we use the word "time" wrongly, we shall end up with the infantile computation of the celebrated Archbishop James Ussher of Armagh, who calculated the earth had its birthday on Saturday, October 22, in 4000 BC, at six in the afternoon … The true age of the sun is perhaps four and a half billion years and subject to revision.'[10]

Christians trust God and the Bible. They believe that God has made it clear that the people in Genesis 5 really existed and that there is a discernable and calculable timeline through the Bible. When the Holy Spirit (the Author of Scripture) repeats himself, it is for emphasis, pointing to important revelation that needs to be believed and remembered (see Gen. 41:32; Acts 10:16). We agree with Professor McIntosh's view regarding the four major genealogies in Scripture: 'When God repeats something we notice it. Three times and we know it is important. Four times and we know there is no doubt that these genealogies are to be treated with the utmost reverence.'[11]

Adam and Eve are regarded as real historic characters, both in the Gospel narratives and in the epistles of the New Testament. Jesus Christ, his apostles and the other authors of the twenty-seven New Testament books teach that God created the world, with the people and events of Genesis 1–11 regarded as history. Jesus himself spoke of:

- '... creation which God created' (Mark 13:19)
- '...the beginning [when God] "made them male and female"' (Matt. 19:4–6; Mark 10:6)
- 'the blood of righteous Abel', the first son of Adam and Eve (Matt. 23:35)
- 'the days of Noah' and the universal Flood (Matt. 24:37; Luke 17:26).

In the epistles of the apostle Peter, we find three references to the worldwide Flood and Noah's ark:

- '... the Divine longsuffering waited in the days of Noah, while the ark was being prepared, in which a few, that is, eight souls, were saved through water' (1 Peter 3:20)
- '[God] did not spare the ancient world, but saved Noah ... bringing in the flood on the world of the ungodly' (2 Peter 2:5)
- '... by the word of God the heavens were of old, and the earth standing out of water and in the water, by which the world that then existed perished, being flooded with water' (2 Peter 3:5–6).

The apostle John had no doubt that Cain, the second son of Adam and Eve, was a real person (1 John 3:12). Other New Testament references to Cain are:

- 'Woe to them! For they have gone in the way of Cain ...' (Jude 11)
- 'By faith Abel offered to God a more excellent sacrifice than Cain' (Heb. 11:4).

Luke wrote a genealogy at the beginning of his Gospel that names the patriarchs and their progenitors as historical persons: 'the son of Jacob, the son of Isaac, the son of Abraham, the son of Terah, the son of Nahor ... the son of Shem, the son of Noah ... the son of Methuselah ... the son of Seth, the son of Adam, the son of God' (Luke 3:34–38). This beloved physician believed in a literal Noah: 'as it was in the days of Noah, so it will be also in the days of the Son of Man' (Luke 17:26).

The apostle Paul made constant reference to the book of Genesis, creation and the events that have shaped the nature and destiny of mankind. Some of Paul's allusions to Genesis are:

- 'God ... commanded light to shine out of darkness' (2 Cor. 4:6). This is a clear reference to Genesis 1:3 and the creation of light on the first day.
- '... as through one man sin entered the world, and death through sin, and thus death spread to all men, because all sinned ...' (Rom. 5:16). This refers back to Genesis 3.
- 'For since by man came death, by Man also came the resurrection of the dead. For as in Adam all die, even so in Christ all shall be made alive' (1 Cor. 15:21–22). This refers back to Genesis 3.
- 'But I fear, lest somehow, as the serpent deceived Eve by his craftiness, so your minds may be corrupted from the simplicity that is in Christ' (2 Cor. 11:3). This refers back to Genesis 3.
- 'For Adam was formed first, then Eve. And Adam was not deceived, but the woman being deceived, fell into transgression' (1 Tim. 2:13–14). This refers back to Genesis 3.

The epistle to the Hebrews makes God the creator of the universe, and chapter 11 takes examples of true faith from the heroes in Genesis 1–11. Hebrews treats the Genesis creation narrative as history, contrasting the historical Jesus with the historical Abel, the son of Adam and Eve:

- 'You, LORD, in the beginning laid the foundation of the earth, and the heavens are the work of Your hands' (Heb. 1:10)
- 'By faith Abel offered to God a more excellent sacrifice than Cain ... By faith Enoch ... did not see death ... By faith Noah ... prepared an ark' (Heb. 11:4–7)
- '... to Jesus the Mediator of the new covenant, and to the blood of sprinkling that speaks better things than that of Abel' (Heb. 12:24).

From the above, an unbiased reader will agree that the Bible leaves us in no doubt that Adam and Eve were regarded as historical characters by Moses, who wrote the book of Genesis, by Jesus Christ, and by the apostolic founders of Christianity. Nor is there any indication of an understanding other than that of six-day creation. The Bible also rules out any suggestion of a 'Gap' or 'Restitution' theory based on Genesis 1:1–3, as there is no record in the New Testament Scriptures of a pre-Adamic catastrophe. The New Testament writers do, however, make much of the worldwide Flood of Noah as recorded in Genesis 6–8.

Proofs for God's existence

Man is made in the image of God (Gen. 1:26), but some reject this truth by suppressing their consciences. Charles Darwin was conscious of God at one time in his life; he said, 'I gradually came to disbelieve in Christianity as a divine revelation ... Thus disbelief crept over me at a very slow rate, but was at last complete.'[12] Darwinians who regard themselves as atheists or agnostics deny and reject the innate—that is, inborn and instinctive—sense of the Almighty in their souls.

When Paul wrote to the Christians at Rome, he had in mind the accounts of God's sovereign judgements recorded in the Old Testament: '... the wrath of God is revealed from heaven against all ungodliness and unrighteousness of men, who suppress the truth in unrighteousness' (Rom. 1:18). These accounts included the worldwide Flood (Gen. 6–8), the destruction of Sodom and Gomorrah (Gen. 19) and the ten plagues of Egypt (Exod. 6–12). He would have regarded these as actual historical events (compare Heb. 11). The wrath of God is God's divine displeasure and indignation against sin. It arises from the divine character, which is holy, and is the determination of the divine mind opposing sin. The effect is to exclude the unrepentant offender from the blessings of the gospel. The sinner is not under God's wrath because of sin alone, for all have sinned (Rom. 3:23), but for failure to repent and be reconciled to God.

God's wrath is still part of the Christian gospel today. It rests on the unbelieving (John 3:36), it is the reward of the ungodly (Col. 3:6) and it is escaped by faith in God's Son, Jesus Christ (1 Thes. 1:10).

Many evolutionists despise these righteous displays of God's character and speak against God with apparently no fear of the judgement to come. Dawkins' outburst is an example: '[God is] a single fiercely unpleasant God, morbidly obsessed with sexual restrictions, with the smell of charred flesh, with his own superiority over rival gods and with the exclusiveness of his chosen desert tribe.'[13] This kind of blasphemy is not new. Two thousand years ago, the ancient Gnostics represented God (whom they called the 'Demiurge') as blind, arrogant, full of envy and the father of death. The Gnostics have now passed into history and most people have never heard of them or their philosophy; likewise Darwinism, with its dependence on so-called science—science that is more religion than knowledge (1 Tim. 6:20)—will, we believe, be forgotten in time. From a biblical point of view, this means that Dawkins and his sort are suppressing their consciences and fighting what is silently being heard within. Although the unconverted soul is without the light of life found in Jesus Christ (John 8:12; 9:5; 12:35) and in spiritual darkness (1 Cor. 2:14), it does not mean that it is without an inborn sense of God. Consider Romans 1:19–22: '… what may be known of God is manifest [plain] in them, for God has shown it to them. For since the creation of the world His invisible attributes are clearly seen … [but] although they knew God, they … became futile in their thoughts, and their foolish hearts were darkened. Professing to be wise, they became fools.'

Here are some questions that arise from these verses:

Q. Do atheists and agnostics have sufficient knowledge of the truth to be aware of the existence of God?

A. Yes, for '… what may be known of God is manifest in them, for God has shown it to them' (v. 19).

Q. Do atheists and agnostics have sufficient knowledge of the truth to acknowledge God as Almighty God?

A. Yes, 'For since the creation of the world His invisible attributes are clearly seen' (v. 20).

Q. Have atheists and agnostics suppressed the knowledge of God they possess?

A. Yes, for 'although they knew God, they … became futile in their thoughts, and their foolish hearts were darkened' (v. 21).

Q. Do atheists and agnostics have sufficient knowledge of the truth to be considered guilty of sinning against light?

A. Yes, for 'Professing to be wise, they became fools' (v. 22).

THE CONSCIENCE

The conscience of fallen man is a 'proof' or 'witness' to God's existence; '... what may be known of God is manifest in them, for God has shown it to them.' Fallen man's conscience speaks truth to his heart even when he hardens and suppresses its voice, as did Pharaoh of old (Exod. 9:34–35). All men and women have a conscience that won't stay silent but is constantly reminding them of right and wrong and of truth and error. The New Testament is uncompromising in its view that man has an innate knowledge of God because God has shown it to man (Rom. 2:14–16); therefore, we are all without excuse (Rom. 1:20). To the Puritan Thomas Watson, man's conscience is the book of the heart; he says, 'The notion of deity is engraved on every man's heart' and 'Conscience is a witness of a Deity. If there were no Bible to tell us there is a God, yet conscience might.'[14]

Creation reveals God's ...	Conscience reveals God's ...
Greatness	Existence
Power	Righteousness
Wisdom	Holiness
Love	Law
Intelligence	Truth
Continuance	Authority

For John Calvin, man's conscience is a sense of the divine judgement. 'It occupies a kind of middle place between God and man, not suffering man to suppress what man knows in himself, but following him out until it bring him to conviction' (Rom. 2:15). It is 'placed over him as a sentinel, to observe and spy out all his secrets, that nothing may remain buried in darkness ... Conscience bears reference to God (as works to men) and hence a good conscience is nothing but inward integrity of heart' (see 1 Tim. 1:5). It differs from intellect. He who sins stands convicted in his conscience before God.[15]

These things being so, Paul wrote that 'Gentiles, who do not have the law, by nature do the things contained in the law' (Rom. 2:14). This is why men and women do things the law of God prescribes; not because they possess a 'selfish gene', as Dawkins suggests, but because the law of God is registered in their consciousness, as the Bible says. They 'show the work of the law written in their hearts, their conscience also bearing witness' (Rom. 2:15). This law is brought to bear upon them by the conscience. So our consciences approve when we do well, but when we go against them, we feel guilty, unless our consciences have been suppressed or seared deliberately by us (Rom. 1:18). The best way to live is to think as the apostle Paul, who said, 'I myself always strive to have a conscience without offense toward God and men' (Acts 24:16).

CREATION *EX NIHILO*

Creation is a 'proof' of God's existence: 'For since the creation of the world his [God's] invisible attributes are clearly seen' (Rom. 1:20). Contrast this with the worldview of the sinner that is twisted and unreliable. Rationalistic philosophy declares human reason to be the final standard, while scepticism says that truth is unattainable. This means that those who deny God's existence and intelligence are deceiving themselves and, for reasons known to themselves, they refuse to acknowledge that God is God. Looking around at the world's beauty and the sky's glory, we see the work of God; the psalmist acknowledged, 'The heavens declare the glory of God; and the firmament shows His handiwork' (Ps. 19:1). General revelation (creation) is so clear an evidence of God's existence that, according to the Bible, it leave us all without excuse (Rom. 1:20).

We asked the question, 'Do atheists and agnostics have sufficient knowledge of the truth to be considered guilty of sinning against light?' and we answered, 'Yes', for the Bible says, 'Professing to be wise, they became fools' (Rom. 1:22).

The book of Hebrews makes one of the Bible's clearest claims about supernatural creation: 'By faith we understand that the worlds were framed by the word of God, so that the things which are seen were not made of things which are visible' (Heb. 11:3).

When God created matter out of nothing (*ex nihilo*), he did not use magic. The supernatural may be mysterious, but creation in six days was not some trick or illusion but the planned omnipotent *work* of God. He created a universe with laws and systems that cosmologists, physicists and

© 2006 Answers in Genesis

others can discover, explore and learn from. The Big Bang is science fiction; creationists have no fear of scientific research that investigates the physics of the cosmos. What Christians object to is religion that is disguised as science by atheists who claim no religion yet propagate unscientific theories with the dogma of extreme fundamentalists.

'Lord, You are God, who made heaven and earth and the sea, and all that is in them' (Acts 4:24).

Notes

1   **Ken Ham,** 'Is Nature the 67th Book of the Bible?', at: ansewrsingenesis.org.

2   The Fellowship of Independent Evangelical Churches (FIEC) Statement of Faith, at: fiec.org.uk.

3   **John Calvin,** Genesis (Edinburgh: Banner of Truth, 1979), p. 94.

4   **Douglas F. Kelly,** Creation and Change : Genesis 1:1–2:4 in the Light of Changing Scientific Paradigms (Fearn: Mentor, 1997), p. 221.

5 **John Byl,** *The Divine Challenge* (Edinburgh: Banner of Truth, 2004), p. 85.

6 **Kelly,** *Creation and Change,* p. 227.

7 Quoted in **Byl,** *The Divine Challenge,* p. 89.

8 **John D. Currid,** *Genesis,* vol. 1 (Darlington: Evangelical Press, 2003), p. 87.

9 **Andy McIntosh,** *Genesis for Today* (Epsom: Day One, 1997), pp. 41–53.

10 **Christopher Hitchens,** *God is Not Great: The Case against Religion* (London: Atlantic Books, 2007), p. 58.

11 **McIntosh,** *Genesis for Today,* p. 51.

12 **Charles Darwin,** *The Autobiography of Charles Darwin , 1809–1882* (London: Collins, 1958), pp. 86–87.

13 **Richard Dawkins,** *The God Delusion* (London: Transworld, 2007), p. 58.

14 **Thomas Watson,** *A Body of Divinity* (London: Banner of Truth, 1970), pp. 41, 55.

15 **John Calvin,** *Institutes,* 4:10:3–4.

Made by God

In the beginning God created the heavens and the earth. (Gen. 1:1)

And the LORD God formed man of the dust of the ground, and breathed into his nostrils the breath of life; and man became a living being. (Gen. 2:7)

For in six days the LORD made the heavens and the earth, the sea, and all that is in them, and rested the seventh day. Therefore the LORD blessed the Sabbath day and hallowed it. (Exod. 20:11)

The truth of the six-day creation of the universe *ex nihilo* (out of nothing) and the Fall of Adam into sin has powerful and continued implications today. Genesis 1–2 emphasize this six-day creation and the seven-day week with a weekly Sabbath rest, while Genesis 3 reveals that God regards all humankind to have sinned in Adam and come short of his glory (Rom. 3:23). Without such truths, there would be no gospel, and without the resurrection of Jesus Christ from the dead, there would be no hope for lost sinners (John 20; 1 Cor. 15). It is important to grasp that, as Henry Morris said, 'The first verse of the Bible—"In the beginning God created the heavens and the earth"—is the foundational verse of the Bible.'[1] Reading Genesis 1–2 gives the clear impression that God made the world in six twenty-four-hour days, that they give an historical account of a chronological progression day after day, and that during this time God saw to it that extraordinary providential care was taken until the work was complete, after which God looked at everything that he had made and saw that it was indeed very good (Gen. 1:31). Thus Genesis teaches creation out of nothing and displays the power and wisdom of Almighty God.

Sadly, there are those who want to read it otherwise. Is what is written in Genesis 1–2 to be taken literally, and how do we know that each day was

A family Bible

twenty-four hours long? Every story has a beginning, and the Bible has something to say about God's world as well as about God himself.

The Hebrew word for 'day'

In the Bible, the Hebrew word translated 'day' is *yôm*; when that word is modified by a number, as in 'first day' or 'third day', it always means twenty-four hours. In Genesis 1, 'evening and morning' equal a twenty-four-hour day. So its normal scriptural usage means a twenty-four-hour solar day.[2] Some liberal scholars agree that the book of Genesis and the Hebrew text *intended* to say six literal days. Professor James Barr, no friend of evangelicals, said in 1984 in a personal letter to David C. C. Watson, 'As far as I know there is no professor of Hebrew or OT at any world-class university who does not believe that the writer of Genesis 1–11 intended to convey to their readers the idea that creation took place in a series of six days which were the same as the days of 24 hours we now experience …'[3]

It is true that sometimes *yôm* is used to signify a general period of time, as in Job 7:6: 'My days are swifter than a weaver's shuttle'; or in Psalm 90:9: 'For all our days have passed away in Your wrath.' But there, *yôm* is linked with the life span of a human being and is not intended to mean millions of years! No such idea (a span of millions of years) fits with the Bible. Leupold says, 'There ought to be no need of refuting the idea that *yôm* means period. Reputable dictionaries … know nothing of this notion. Hebrew dictionaries are our primary source of reliable information concerning Hebrew words.'[4]

POETRY?

Some people want to regard Genesis 1 as poetry, but there is no indication in the Hebrew text that it is either poetry or allegory. There is no indication that the narrative is meant to be understood in a non-literal, non-historical or non-chronological way; instead, the opposite is true, as the text is straightforward historical narrative. To indicate this, the Hebrew in Genesis 1 uses a grammatical device called the '*waw*-consecutive-plus-imperfect'.[5] *Waw* is the letter 'w' in biblical Hebrew and is used to indicate events happening in sequence; it appears throughout Hebrew narrative. It is placed before the imperfect verb, becoming the first letter of the word. The second edition of *Gesenius' Hebrew Grammar* says, 'The progress in sequence of time is regularly indicated by a pregnant "and" (called *waw consecutive*).'[6]

This grammatical device is used in Hebrew prose but not in Hebrew poetry, proving that Genesis should be read as clear-cut history. It has been said, 'This is awkward in English, but good Hebrew.'[7] That Genesis 1 is narrative and not poetry is also indicated by the omission of figurative language such as metaphors. In addition, the most basic feature of biblical Hebrew poetry is line parallelism, when the second line essentially says the same thing as the first line. This is a crucial feature of Hebrew poetry but is not found in Genesis 1.[8]

In six days

The idea of chance random processes and long ages is alien to the book of Genesis and therefore the message of Genesis is contrary to Darwinism. In Genesis 1:2, we see everything as being under the control of God the Holy Spirit. There was Trinitarian work at the beginning of time, when 'the Spirit of God was hovering over the face of the waters'. He hovered over the formless (Hebrew *tohu*) emptiness (Hebrew *bohu*) as an eagle hovers over its young (Deut. 32:11). He was there at the origin of the cosmos. Only the Hebrew Scriptures say that light preceded the sun in creation, so this idea was therefore not copied from other sources; neither does the Bible regard Genesis 1–2 as a fable, as the creation story is repeated through the whole of the Old Testament.

The idea of light before the creation of the sun is so unexpected that it verges on the incomprehensible. In Genesis 1:14, God said, 'Let there be lights in the firmament of the heavens to divide the day from the night; and let them be for signs and seasons, and for days and years.' The lights (sun and moon) were given for signs, for seasons, days and years on Day 4; this indicates that the days were of twenty-four-hour duration, for if the 'days' were long ages, what, then, are the years? According to Genesis 1:14–19, the sun and moon were made on Day 4, so the Bible has its own unique view of origins. Evolutionists reckon that the moon was formed as the result of an impact between a large meteor the size of Mars and the earth about 4.4

Big Bang	Stars	Sun	Molten Earth	First Oceans
15 Billion years ago	10 Billion years ago	5 Billion years ago	4.5 Billion years ago	3.8 Billion years ago
Water covered Earth	Dry land and plants	Sun, moon, and stars	Sea and flying creatures	Land animals and Man
Day 1-2	Day 3	Day 4	Day 5	Day 6

billion years ago, first forming a single clump of rock and then 'evolving' into a spherical rock a year after the impact![9] Conversely, the young-earth creation model demonstrates that our moon is in the exact place it needs to be by God's design and is the perfect distance from the earth (384,403 km) to be of help with tides and oceanic drift. This was a deliberate act of our Creator God; Day 4 was a solar day of twenty-four hours. Our moon is about a quarter of the size of the earth and rotates around its own axis while it orbits the earth at 3,683 km per hour, while the earth rotates at 1,600 km per hour. Psalm 136:5–9 is clear about God's creation of the sun to light the world: '… by wisdom [God] made the heavens… [and] made *great lights* … the sun to rule by day… the moon and stars to rule by night.' These two great lights were made at the same time and were ordained (decreed) by God himself. He fixed them in the heavens permanently for a specific task: the sun to rule by day and the moon and the stars to rule by night (Jer. 31:35). The sun and moon were part of his predetermined plan for the sustaining of life and were specifically and supernaturally created when he made the universe. The world is controlled by God's decrees as the laws of nature (see Job 28:26; Prov. 8:29), which 'work all things according to the counsel of His will' (Eph. 1:11). The decrees of God are seated in his wisdom (Ps. 104:24; Prov. 3:19). Without eyewitnesses to the creation event, humanity can only speculate about the beginning or accept the alternative, which is to believe the Bible. The Bible claims to be an eyewitness account, and we are expected to believe it, for God was there (Gen. 1:2)!

DAYS 5 AND 6

The Bible is not a book just about God; it is also about the world he created out of nothing. It records what happened in the past, at the beginning of time, revealing both his power and his plan. The alternative to believing the Bible is to believe in the doctrinaire atheistic ideological scientific hypothesis known today as Darwinism.

Darwinian evolutionists say that fish evolved into amphibians, which, in turn, produced birds over millions of years; but the Bible says that birds were made on Day 5 and the reptiles on Day 6, contradicting these ideas:

- Day 5: 'God said, "Let the waters abound with an abundance of living creatures"' (Gen. 1:20). Evolutionary scientists claim that fish have changed over time to produce new species; however, after intensive experimentation over 100 years, fish still remain fish!
- Day 5: 'God created … every winged bird according to its kind' (Gen. 1:21).
- Day 6: 'God made the beast of the earth according to its kind, and everything that creeps on the earth' (Gen. 1:25).

The Bible gives God the credit for the creation of man on Day 6 (Gen. 1:26–27). Man was the highest of all God's works, and the psalmist noted this when he wrote, 'For You have made him a little lower than the angels, and You have crowned him with glory and honor' (Ps. 8:5). Man (Adam) was made in God's image; this view of the dignity of mankind as taught in the Bible is contrary to that of the Darwinian mindset that regards human beings merely as higher animals with no destiny or eternal hope. But the Bible is clear: 'God said, "Let Us make man in Our image, according to Our likeness"' (Gen. 1:26). Man was to be different from the other creatures (*nephesh*) (Gen. 1:20).[10] He was to be dignified (Ps. 8:5), having personality, moral purity and spiritual ability to talk to God.

'... in the image of God He created him; male and female He created them' (Gen. 1:27). Man and woman were to be in the likeness of God, image-bearers in righteousness and true holiness. From the beginning, there was Adam and Eve, not Adam and Steve! The account of the creation of Eve is not what evolutionists want to read, for there is no way this fits into their theory of origins. The New Testament backs up the Genesis account: 'For Adam was formed first, then Eve' (1 Tim. 2:13). All other women were born of women, but the first woman was made from man (Gen. 2:21–22). The Puritan Matthew Henry, commenting on Genesis 2:21–22, said that Eve was 'not made out of his head to rule over him, nor out of his feet to be trampled upon by him, but out of his side to be equal with him, under his arm to be protected, and near his heart to be beloved'.[11]

'And the LORD God formed man of the dust of the ground, and breathed into his nostrils the breath of life; and man became a living being' (Gen. 2:7). God used the basic chemical elements as the physical building blocks of the human body. It is a sobering thought that 'dust you are, and to dust you shall return' (Gen. 3:19).

In the New Testament, Jesus Christ mentions the death of Abel, the son of Adam and Eve, thereby confirming the history of man's origin (Matt. 23:35), and the apostle Paul accepted the historicity of Adam, saying, 'The first man was of the earth, made of dust' (1 Cor. 15:47). Man's origin did not come about by chance, nor was it the product of millions of years of change; rather it was the product of a moment of supernatural activity by Almighty God. Man is made in the image and according to the likeness of God. Man is clearly patterned after his Maker and so is a child of God. God is the Potter, and we are the clay. Darwinian natural selection is a hypothesis that just does not fit with the Bible. The only places where frogs become human beings are in fairytales and in the minds of evolutionists.

EXODUS 20

Are there any other passages in the Bible that speak of a sequential, chronological creation? Yes; Exodus 20 shows that the seven-day week is rooted in the creation account of Genesis 1–2. In his book *Genesis for Today*, Professor Andy McIntosh says, 'The most conclusive of all arguments concerning the days of Genesis 1 being literal 24-hour periods is to be found in Exodus 20:8–11 … The creation ordinance, repeated by Moses in this passage, is that man is to keep every seventh 24-hour period—not every seventh week or century!'[12] When the ordinary reader is told that Day 1 of the creation account led to Day 2 and eventually to Day 7 in a chronological way, he or she is entitled to believe it to have been so.

The seventh day

The seven-day week speaks of creation *ex nihilo*. Why is there a seven-day week? This is a question that has puzzled many. Agnostic Darwinians appear to be ambivalent about Sunday's origin and its importance, and they do not discuss it; as a result, they have neglected arguing against what is an important proof for six-day creation.[13] It is not adequate to end the creation story on the sixth day, no matter how important it is to emphasize six literal days. This is because there is one more day in the week that the Lord God made: 'And on the seventh day God ended His work which He had done' (Gen. 2:2). The week is the standard model of time, and we find its origin in biblical history. The cycle of seven days bears no relation to the moon's rotation round the earth or the orbit of the earth round the sun. God had already finished his work of creation by the end of the sixth day and so abstained from work on the seventh day. The seventh day was made to be different. John Owen said, 'Some peculiar good was added unto it.'[14] Thus appears the distinction between the six days of labour and the one of rest. If the six days of Genesis 1 are long ages, how long is the Sabbath day?

In Exodus 20 we have the giving of the Ten Commandments by Moses. The fourth commandment agrees with the Bible's creation account in Genesis 1–2 (that creation *ex nihilo* took six twenty-four-hour days). Thus the children of Israel were reminded that the Sabbath day was also an ordinary day of twenty-four hours: '… in six days the LORD made the heavens and the earth, the sea, and all that is in them, and rested the seventh day. Therefore the LORD blessed the Sabbath day and hallowed it' (Exod. 20:11).

But is there a reason why God took this length of time? He could have taken six seconds to make the cosmos, or six minutes, or six years, or six million years, if he had so chosen. So why six days? Two reasons stand out.

The *first* is to teach humankind that twenty-four hours is the length of the Sabbath day and a Sabbath's rest. As Bruce Ray has commented, 'The week was established by the sovereign appointment of the Creator, and from the very beginning God arranged the lives of his people around the Sabbath.'[15]

God made time. Time does not exist independently but is the product of the creation week. Thus the hebdomadal (seven-day) cycle goes back to Genesis 1–2 and not to the Babylonians or the Greeks. The weekly pattern of six days work and one day rest is God's idea. God blessed the seventh day and made it holy (Gen. 2:2–3), thus the seven-day week was born. God established a pattern for man to follow. Douglas F. Kelly puts it this way: 'Apparently mankind is so important to the infinite God that He arranged His creative activity specifically to set the structure for human life. That must be a major reason why God created over six days, rather than in a split second (or a hundred billion years).'[16]

So God took six days over creation for humanity's benefit and for its prosperity, dignity and unity. It was an act of love as well as power; an act of condescension as well as glory. Sabbath rest is a pattern to be followed, a provision to be welcomed and a gift to be prized. Atheistic evolutionists hate the concept of a creator God because they do not like to be dictated to by the Bible. Because of the Fall, they would rather disobey God's commands than humbly accept the Creator's plans for them (Rom 1:20). This results in a rejection of the Christian Sabbath as a day of rest.

> Remember the Sabbath day, to keep it holy
> (Ex. 20:8).

That God rested on the seventh day is evidence that we are to rest also; the whole day is to be kept holy. But evolutionary theory undermines this principle among God's people. Thus there is a need for a high view of Scripture that upholds the creation account as historically accurate and therefore proclaims Sunday to be a day of rest for believers and for all people. Why do we say this? We do so because Jesus Christ said, 'The Sabbath was made for man, and not man for the Sabbath' (Mark 2:27). However, many believers today seem overwhelmed by a secular view of Sunday that ignores what the Bible says about the Christian Sabbath, so they adopt a view that, like Darwinism, rejects the need for one day in seven as a day for rest and worship. If the universe was not created in six literal days, it is hard to understand the reasoning behind the argument for a Sabbath rest one day in seven. All efforts by atheists to secularize society aids the plan to remove from memory the uniqueness and the glorious brevity of the creation account. Not content with what has already been achieved in this matter, the devil wants to finish the job. So-called science and Darwinism are tools to this end.

The *second* reason for six-day creation is that it is a proof of God's existence, as the New Testament makes clear: 'For since the creation of the world His [God's] invisible attributes are clearly seen' (Rom. 1:20). This means that those who deny God's existence and intelligence are deceiving themselves when they refuse to acknowledge that God is God. Beholding the world's beauty and the sky's glory, we see the work of God; this is what the psalmist acknowledged: 'The heavens declare the glory of God; and the firmament shows His handiwork' (Ps. 19:1). General revelation (creation) is so clear an evidence of God's existence that, according to the Bible, it leave us all without excuse (Rom. 1:20). The book of Hebrews makes one of the Bible's clearest claims about supernatural creation: 'By faith we understand that the worlds were framed by the word of God, so that the things which are seen were not made of things which are visible' (Heb. 11:3).

When God created matter out of nothing, he did not use magic. The supernatural may be mysterious, but creation in six days was not some trick or illusion; rather it was the planned omnipotent work of God. When he said, 'Let there be light', we understand his will, and when we read, 'and there was light', we read of his work.

- Only God can create out of nothing.
- Only Intelligence can design and manufacture.
- Only life can beget life.

God created a universe with laws and systems that cosmologists, physicists and others can discover, explore and learn from. Speaking of the Holy Spirit's part in creation, H. C. Leupold says, 'We should not be averse to holding that the foundation of all physical laws operative in the world now was laid by this preparatory activity.'[17]

Notes

1 **H. M. Morris,** *The Genesis Record* (Grand Rapids, MI: Baker, 1998), p. 37.

2 For a full discussion on this see 'Could God have Created Everything in Six Days?', **Ken Ham** *et al., The New Answers Book* (Green Forest, AR: Master Books, 2007), pp. 88–112.

3 Quoted in **Douglas F. Kelly,** *Creation and Change : Genesis 1:1–2:4 in the Light of Changing Scientific Paradigms* (Fearn: Mentor, 1997), p. 51.

4 **H. C. Leupold,** *Exposition of Genesis* (London: Evangelical Press, 1972), p. 57.

5 **John D. Currid,** *Genesis,* vol. 1 (Darlington: Evangelical Press, 2003), p. 38.

6 **H. F. W. Gesenius, E. Kautzsch** and **A. E. Cowley,** (eds.), *Gesenius' Hebrew Grammar* (USA: Oxford University Press, 1922), p. 133.

7 See **S. E. Waldron,** *A Modern Exposition of the 1689 Baptist Confession of Faith* (Darlington: Evangelical Press, 1999), pp. 78, 477, n. 4 regarding the refutation of the day–age theory.

8 **Currid,** *Genesis,* p. 39.

9 **Bill Bryson,** *A Short History of Nearly Everything* (London: Transworld, 2004), p. 62.

10 *Nephesh* speaks of the 'animating principle of the body, and is the common property of man and beast'. **R. B. Girdlestone,** *Synonyms of the Old Testament* (Grand Rapids, MI: W. B. Eerdmans, 1978), p. 56.

11 **Matthew Henry,** *Commentary on the Whole Bible,* vol. 1 (Glasgow: Pickering and Ingles), p. 20.

12 **Andy McIntosh,** *Genesis for Today* (Epsom: Day One, 1997), p. 39.

13 There is nothing in Bryson, Dawkins or Hitchens about it.

14 **John Owen,** *The Works of John Owen,* **W. H. Goold,** (ed.), vol. 18 (Edinburgh: Banner of Truth, 1977), p. 332.

15 **Bruce A. Ray,** *Celebrating the Sabbath* (Phillipsburg, NJ: Presbyterian & Reformed, 2000), pp. 15–16.

16 **Kelly,** *Creation and Change,* p. 109.

17 **Leupold,** *Exposition of Genesis,* p. 50.

Theistic evolution

Where were you when I laid the foundations of the earth? (Job 38:4)

Then God said, 'Let Us make man in Our image, according to Our likeness.' (Gen. 1:26)

The LORD by wisdom founded the earth; by understanding He established the heavens; by His knowledge the depths were broken up, and clouds drop down the dew ... (Prov. 3:19–20)

What do evangelical Christians believe when it comes to the theory of evolution? Are we happy with the comment from Alistair McGrath that 'there is no difficulty, for example, in believing that Darwin's theory of evolution is presently the best explanation of the available [scientific] evidence'?[1] Are the 'days' of Genesis 1–2 literal, and are they real twenty-four-hour days? If so, it would directly contradict the theory of evolution and Charles Darwin's attempt to undermine the Christian faith that is founded on God's Word alone. Francis Schaeffer said that creation was 'the first category that many churches either failed or refused to recognise'. This is because the lostness of the sinner is 'answered by the existence of a Creator'. So Christianity does not begin with accepting Christ as Saviour but with 'In the beginning God created the heavens and the earth' (Gen. 1:1). Schaeffer also felt that we are greatly mistaken to avoid the important subject of 'How did we get here?' He thought that when we avoid this question, which is deeply implanted in every human heart, Christians jump immediately to salvation and so 'lose the major impact on those who are seeking the truth'.[2]

Science against God

What is science? This is a fundamental question in the creation/evolution

Many say that "six days" is a side issue because on that issue, they've joined the other side.

Which side do you choose?

© 2006 Answers in Genesis

debate; if 'science' is not defined clearly, much of what is said on the topic is not relevant, and much that is relevant, from a young-earth creationist point of view, needs to be constantly repeated in order to get the point across. Experimental and observable (empirical) science is not questioned by young-earth creationists; it is the speculative and doctrinaire side of science that is found wanting, in their opinion. In fact, such science is more like a religion than a provable discipline. Science cannot directly deal with the past; it cannot go back in time and experiment. The New Testament alerts us to beware of the 'profane and idle babblings and contradictions of what is falsely called knowledge' (1 Tim. 6:20) and the 'hollow and deceptive philosophy, which depends on human tradition' (Col. 2:8). What needs to be remembered is that much evolutionary teaching is founded on an atheistic view of life, and this colours the conclusions that are drawn when theories about origins are proposed.

The problem of design is recognized by evolutionists. Richard Dawkins, in his usual dismissive way, makes light of the concept of intelligent design, saying it is 'an argument that could only be made by someone who doesn't understand the first thing about natural selection'.3 But is this really so? The Bible is full of claims that it was the Trinitarian God who designed and created the universe and placed mankind on the earth. Thus the work of creation is attributed to all three Persons of the Trinity (Gen. 1:1; Isa. 40:26; Ps. 104:30a; Acts 17:24; Col. 1:6).

The New Testament view of the universe is very different from the Darwinian theory of the origin of matter as it clearly says that Jesus Christ is Creator of all things (John 1:1–3; Col. 1:15–16). Not only was he responsible for creating all things but, according to the New Testament, the universe was made *for* him: 'For by Him all things were created that are in heaven and that are on earth, visible and invisible … All things were created through Him and for Him. And He is before all things, and in Him all things consist' (Col. 1:16–17).

Many see the issue of creation and origins as science against God. This antagonism is generated by the constant reports of newly discovered fossils in daily newspapers, secular magazines and on TV news programmes, which view and discuss them from an evolutionary point of view. Dinosaurs and other creatures are reported to have existed millions of years ago, and sea monsters like the 15-metre-long Pliosaur (a type of Plesiosaur), whose fossil was discovered recently in Norway and dated at 150 million years old, are typical examples of Darwinian propaganda.4

Another reason why the theory of evolution is assumed to be valid is because it is taught in our schools and universities as fact. It is evident that very many who have gone through higher education are running scared of their peers when it comes to challenging Darwinism, even when evolution still remains a hypothesis and an unproven assumption. On the other hand, Bible Christians believe what the Scriptures say about God and origins as well as what they say about Jesus Christ and salvation. Douglas Kelly reminds us in his book *Creation and Change*, 'The Bible does not start with an apology nor with an argument, it simply starts with God.'5

Does science make belief in God obsolete? This question has been the subject of recent debate and a series of thirteen short essays, published by the Templeton Foundation in 2008, offers different responses. That it is asked at all shows how agnostic our once-Christian society has become. Several scientists answered 'No' to the question, but one response was telling; indeed, it stands out. This response came from Kenneth Miller, theistic evolutionist and a professor at Brown University. He said,

The categorical mistake of the atheist is to assume that God is natural and therefore within the realm of science to investigate and test. By making God an ordinary part of the natural world, and failing to find him there, they conclude that he does not exist. But God is not and cannot be part of nature. God is the reason for nature, the explanation of why things are. He is the answer to existence, not part of existence itself.[6]

Theology teaches that God is transcendent and separate from his creation and the restraints of physics and time. This is partly what the psalmist meant when he wrote, '[You] have set Your glory above the heavens!' (Ps. 8:1).

Evolutionists believe that the universe appeared after the Big Bang some 14.2 billion years ago. There are two Big Bang models of the universe which hold sway today. The inflationary model posits a particle of matter so small that it was almost nothing in size and weighed 1 ounce; it is

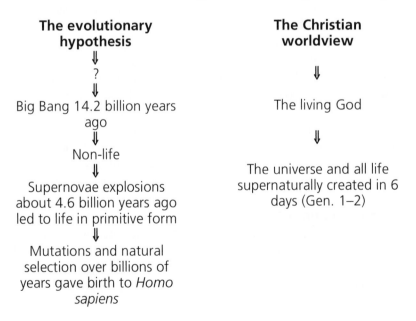

The evolutionary hypothesis	The Christian worldview
⇓	
?	⇓
⇓	
Big Bang 14.2 billion years ago	The living God
⇓	⇓
Non-life	
⇓	The universe and all life supernaturally created in 6 days (Gen. 1–2)
Supernovae explosions about 4.6 billion years ago led to life in primitive form	
⇓	
Mutations and natural selection over billions of years gave birth to *Homo sapiens*	

described as being a billionth of the size of a proton, which is itself 500th of a billionth of the size of the dot on this 'i'. The older Big Bang model theorizes a spot 'so infinitesimally compact that it has no dimensions at all'.[7] So evolutionists believe that, from an infinitesimally small particle, 'in less than a minute the universe is a million billion miles across and growing fast … in three minutes, 98 per cent of all matter there is or will ever be has been produced'.[8] But the Big Bang was not enough! The author Bill Bryson is honest enough to tell us that the Big Bang theory has one gaping hole: 'namely that it could not explain how we got here'![9] This is because the Big Bang supposedly created light gases such as helium, hydrogen and lithium, but no heavy elements; 'Not one particle of the heavy stuff so vital to our being—carbon, nitrogen, oxygen and all the rest—emerged from the gaseous brew of creation.'[10] So what is missing from this theory that has been adopted as truth by billions of our fellow humans all over the world? It is smaller 'big bangs'! These were in the form of exploding supernovae (very large stars). The hypothesis suggests that the exploding stars produced the necessary missing elements—called interstellar medium—to build a universe that could, if things went well, create a planet like Earth, which, if chance random processes fell out in man's favour, would result in animal and human life as we see it today. When did this happen? It is postulated that some 4.6 billion years ago (i.e. 9.6 billion years after the Big Bang), the earth began to form and after 200 million years was still molten but large enough to be called a planet.

However, two questions must be asked: (i) If the second 'big bang' was necessary to create our sun, where did the supernovae come from? (ii) Why is it that little is heard of these supernovae when this theory is explained at popular level? These ideas were first mooted by Sir Fred Hoyle in 1957. We suggest that the reason why this is not clearly and openly discussed is because it makes the theory awkward and apparently less likely to be believed.

Old-earth creationists

Old-earth creationists are also known as 'day–age theorists' because they equate the days of creation with the long ages of Darwinism. Some have gone to great lengths to try to reconcile the views of the Bible with non-empirical science or to make a division between science and theology. One

Helix nebula

such in the 19th century was Dr James Woodrow. Of Scottish descent, he came originally from Carlisle but his family emigrated to Canada and then to Ohio, USA, when he was eight years old. Woodrow struggled with three things: (i) the age of the earth; (ii) the unity of the human race; and (iii) the extent of Noah's flood. He was a Professor of Natural History and an

American Presbyterian theologian ordained into the ministry in 1859 who tried to make a 'radical division between science and theology'. This resulted in a bitter and extended struggle in his denomination, the Southern Presbyterian Church of North America, in the late 19th century. Woodrow claimed that the Bible was completely silent on all scientific matters and was not intended to be a textbook of science, saying that the Bible 'can only speak incidentally about scientific matters, and such information is of no help to science'.[11] His endeavour to make the Bible subordinate to so-called scientific explanations of the origins of the universe—which are always changing—was in essence an attempt to keep intellectual respectability within the academic world as well as to silence the Word of God on the topic of origins on which it is specifically clear.

Why is it incorrect to say that the Darwinian evolutionary hypothesis is an option when assessing the age of the universe? Theistic evolution suggests that God used the Big Bang to make matter and the earth as we find it today. What is wrong with this idea as a solution to where we came from?

Firstly, it clearly contradicts the views of the Psalms, several of which speak of a transcendent creator God (see, for example, Ps. 8:3–8; 19:1–6; 33:6–9; 74:15–17; 90:2; 102:25–26; 104:5–9, 30; 136:5–9). Secondly, knowledge of God would be impossible if he had not revealed his existence to us through the Bible. We can learn about God from his creation, as Psalm 19 demonstrates: 'The heavens declare the glory of God; and the firmament shows His handiwork' (Ps. 19:1). But true knowledge of God comes only from special revelation, under the illumination of the Holy Spirit. God can be known only as he actively makes himself known. He is the *Subject* of the Bible—he communicates knowledge. He is also the *Object*—he is known through the knowledge conveyed to us in revelation; therefore, if there is no revelation, there is no knowledge of God. Through revelation, God is *actively* making himself known—it is a supernatural act of self-communication.[12]

Other theistic theories

THE GAP THEORY

The Gap Theory is another hypothesis suggested to get around the literal reading of Genesis. It is an attempt to reconcile Genesis 1 with scientific objections to a young earth. A 'gap' of millions of years is theorized between verses 1 and 2 of Genesis 1:1–2: '¹In the beginning God created the heavens and the earth. ²The earth was without form, and void …'

This theory speculates that, between these two verses, the fall and rebellion of Satan took place, resulting in millions of years of death and bloodshed before the creation of Adam and Eve. The theory holds that God then destroyed the original creation in judgement, and it suggests that verse 2a gives a statement of a ruined cosmos ('without form, and void'), while verse 2b speaks of a 'second creation', the Holy Spirit being its originator and with Adam and Eve as the new parents of all mankind. This was God attempting to do things better a second time! This theory places the beginning of creation week in verse 2b—'and the Spirit of God was hovering over the face of the waters'—and not in verse 1—'In the beginning God created the heavens and the earth'. This exegesis was an attempt by theistic evolutionists to reconcile and accommodate the vast geological ages spoken of by Darwinian geologists.

The Gap Theory originated from a Scottish Presbyterian evangelical theologian, Dr Thomas Chalmers (1780–1847); although he is credited with its inception, he actually said very little about it in his writings. This hypothesis, which is sometimes also called the 'restitution theory' or the 'ruin-and-reconstruction theory', was popular in some conservative circles in the late 19th and early 20th centuries, when evangelicals such as Arthur W. Pink thought it helpful to suggest it to the readers of their writings.[13] They, like Dr Chalmers, were making an attempt to fit 19th-century 'scientific' explanations of geological discoveries into the Bible's timeline.

Thomas Chalmers

However, they were reading into Scripture what is not there, so the hypothesis was doomed to fail; it pleased neither evolutionists nor those who preferred the plain reading of Scripture to prevail.

The Gap Theory holds that all things except Adam and Eve were made before the six-day creation and that the sun existed before Day 4, an explicit contradiction to the creation account in Genesis 1:14–19. Those who accept the authority of Scripture cannot accept this idea. As Ken Ham has said, 'All versions of the gap theory impose outside ideas on Scripture and thus open the door for further compromise.'14

THE FRAMEWORK HYPOTHESIS

The Framework Hypothesis suggests that Genesis 1 should be interpreted topically, not chronologically. Proponents of this theory want to interpret it in the light of Genesis 2, contending that 'Genesis 2 is marked by a highly structured style and has thematic parallels with chapter 1'.15 The main spokesman for this theory was Meredith Kline (1922–2007), who developed a view that suggested that the creation account in Genesis 1 is poetic and so must not be understood as sequential. There is no exegetical basis for saying there is a contradiction between the creation accounts of Genesis 1 and 2; the idea hinges on 2:4–7:

This is the history of the heavens and the earth when they were created, in the day that the LORD God made the earth and the heavens, before any plant of the field was in the earth and before any herb of the field had grown. For the LORD God had not caused it to rain on the earth, and there was no man to till the ground … And the LORD God formed man of the dust of the ground, and breathed into his nostrils the breath of life; and man became a living being.

What we have in Genesis 2 is not the origin but the subsequent history of the heavens and the earth. It is a sequel to chapter 1 and not a second account of creation. Those who advocate the Framework Hypothesis wish to bring in the idea of *normal* providential activity at creation of the world; however, the Bible records a *supernatural* creation of mankind. Joseph Pipa puts it this way: 'Just as extraordinary providence works alongside regular providence in history, we may assume God operated the same way during creation.'16 God is reported in Genesis to have supernaturally made the universe in six days out of nothing.

PROGRESSIVE CREATIONISM

Progressive Creationism has been promoted in recent times by Hugh N. Ross, the president and founder of Reasons to Believe, an organization located in Pasadena, California, which deals with apologetics.[17] Hugh Ross defines Progressive Creationism as 'the hypothesis that God has increased the complexity of life on earth by successive creations of new life forms over billions of years while miraculously changing the earth to accommodate the new life'.[18] Progressive Creationism holds that:

- The earth and the universe are billions of years old.
- The days of creation were overlapping periods of millions of years.
- Death and bloodshed have existed from the beginning of creation and were not the result of Adam's sin.
- Man was created after the vast majority of earth's history of life and death had already taken place.
- The Flood of Noah's time was local and not global, although it did kill all humans outside the ark.
- Earth's geology represents billions of years of history.

This idea is popular among those who are intimidated by Darwinism. Ross cannot put millions of years into the biblical timeline, so he has invented a theory that purports that 'people' before Adam had no soul. His ideas are as follows:

Starting about 2–4 million years ago, God began creating man like mammals or hominoids. They stood on two feet and used tools; some even buried their dead. However, they were very different from us. They had no spirit and they did not have a conscience like we have. In time, these hominoid-like creatures became extinct. Then, about 10–25 thousand years ago, God replaced them with Adam and Eve.[19]

This is an example of a Christian trying to accommodate Darwinism and at the same time be true to the Scriptures, but it simply does not work. We are left with the obvious questions: How could Ross know that these hypothetical hominoids had no soul or conscience? Has he dug one up? If so, was it accompanied with a note saying, 'I have no soul or conscience so God got rid of me'? Where does Ross get these ideas? Surely he is hypothesizing simply in order to accommodate Darwinian notions and the theories of survival of the fittest and natural selection over millions of years.

'OLD EARTH, YOUNG ADAM' CREATIONISTS

Another hypothesis that is gaining support among theistic evolutionists is that which talks of an old earth and a young Adam and Eve. This theory is invented to cope with the immense gap and obvious contradiction between what the Bible says in Genesis 1–2 about the universe (including the creation of Adam and Eve) being created *ex nihilo* in six twenty-four-hour days and what Darwinians postulate as the long ages required to achieve the evolution of man from the Big Bang (which is around 14.2 billion years). Six days or 14.2 billion years: there can be no agreement between these two ideas, yet this is what 'old earth, young Adam' theorists want to achieve.

They argue that man is unique and made in God's image, but that this was achieved through evolution. Sometime in the evolutionary timescale—no one can pinpoint where or when—God separated two hominoid creatures who at some point in the evolutionary process had developed a God consciousness; God called them Adam and Eve. They were endued with the communicable attributes of deity so as to be 'made in his image'. The Garden of Eden was never real but simply illustrative of God's care of Adam and Eve in a fallen world; death and bloodshed were constant features of the evolutionary method before this moment.

Genesis tells us that man was created in God's image—'male and female He created them' (Gen. 1:27)—but according to old-earthers, Adam and Eve evolved from a single cell by chance random processes through death and bloodshed over millions of years. Thus their 'Adam' and 'Eve' were not genetically related, as Genesis 2:21–22 claims (no supernatural creation of Eve from Adam's side), but the two evolved as separate individuals who presumably mated at some point in the evolutionary process while surrounded by millions of other Neanderthals like them!

Those who know the Bible can see straight away what is wrong with these ideas. For example, they:

- contract the plain reading of the book of Genesis
- ignore the other portions of the Old and New Testaments that support six-day creation and a literal Garden of Eden (e.g. Exod. 20:11; Rom. 5:12–14)
- ignore the historic event of the Fall in the Garden of Eden and do not know where this happened, if it happened at all

- ignore that Eve was made from Adam's side (Gen. 2:21–23; 1 Cor. 11:8)
- make nonsense of the Genesis 3 and New Testament accounts of the Fall, which need a tree of the knowledge of good and evil and a tree of life, a serpent (Satan) and angelic cherubim, as well as a perfect Adam and Eve (Gen. 3; Matt. 19:4–6; Rom. 5:12–21; 1 Cor. 11:8; 15:45; 1 Tim. 2:13–14)
- call into question the existence of the devil himself
- reject the post-creation, pre-Fall covenant made between God and Adam (Gen. 2:15–17)[20]
- contradict Jesus Christ's acceptance of Adam as the first man made in God's image at the beginning of creation (Matt. 19:4; 23:35; Mark 10:6)
- deny that Adam and Eve were supernaturally created in the image of God as described in Genesis 1–2
- ignore the Bible genealogies, which make clear that Adam was the first man and had human descendents (Gen. 5)
- imply that true religion begins in Genesis 11, with Abraham, rather than with Abel, the first son of Adam and Eve at the beginning of time (Heb. 11:4; 12:24)
- deny the doctrine of biblical headship which is based on the premise that Adam was created first, then Eve (1 Cor. 11:8–12)
- call into question the whole story of redemption and the need for the last Adam and the second man (Matt. 1:18–25; Luke 1:26–38; 1 Cor. 15:45).

Old-earthers know that their ideas do not fit with the Bible, so why do they persist in holding them? We suggest it is because they are willing to give way to the present views of secular naturalism, irrespective of the implications for the veracity of Scripture. If they continue to do so, their ideas will lead to the destroying of evangelical Protestant Christianity, which holds to the inerrancy of the Bible.[21]

A careful and trusting examination of the biblical text is the way to see off this hypothesis. We must understand and interpret Scripture by Scripture; this is one of the cardinal rules of biblical hermeneutics.

Genesis ruined!

One theistic evolutionist is Don Stoner, who, when looking at Genesis 1, interprets it in the light of what he thinks scientists have been able to learn about God's creation; he deals with the text of Scripture as a secondary source, making its meaning dependent on the most recent scientific knowledge and theories. He does so, admitting that he is attempting 'to correlate present-day theories with the Bible'. Where does this attempt lead him?

On this basis, Stoner says of the word 'earth' in Genesis 1:1 ('In the beginning God created the heavens and the *earth*') that 'this verse could refer to cosmic matter in the general sense—the matter from which the earth, stars and planets were ultimately formed'.[22] Continuing to interpret Genesis 1 in a similar way, he says:

DAY 1

- Genesis 1:1 is equivalent to 15–20 billion years ago.
- Genesis 1:2 is equivalent to about 4.5 billion years ago.
- Genesis 1:3 is equivalent to about 4.5 billion years ago.

DAY 2

- Genesis 1:6–8 is equivalent to about 4 billion years ago.

DAY 3

- Genesis 1:9–10 is equivalent to 2.5–3 billion years ago.
- Genesis 1:11–13 is equivalent to possibly 1–2 billion years ago.

DAY 4

- Genesis 1:14–19 is equivalent to possibly 1 billion years ago.

DAY 5

- Genesis 1:20–23 is equivalent to about 500–600 million years ago.

DAY 6

- Genesis 1:24–25 is equivalent to about 230 million years ago.
- Genesis 1:26–27 is equivalent to possibly 40 thousand years ago.[23]

While upholding that God himself created the universe, Stoner makes the mistake of believing that it is the scientist who will help us understand how awesome God is, when he should understand that it is the Bible that grants us a full revelation of God while his creation illustrates his power, wisdom and eternal Godhead (Ps. 19).

Some old-earth creationists want to posit the idea that pre-existent matter was at hand before God got to work in six-day creation; they therefore depart from the normal English translation in Genesis 1:1 and render it 'when God *began* to create'.[24] This is not acceptable because such a translation renders verse 1 as a temporal and not an absolute clause, suggesting a connection between the so-called Babylonian creation account *Enuma Elish* and the Genesis version. However, the Bible's account of creation in six days is very different from this Mesopotamian document or other near-Eastern magic-filled drama accounts of creation; the Bible depicts a sovereign God creating the universe *ex nihilo*, then resting on the seventh day as a perpetual sign of the seven-day week. The Hebrew text indicates clearly that God was at work, as E. J. Young says with reference to the Hebrew word translated 'create': 'If in Genesis 1:1 Moses desired to express the thought of absolute creation, there was no more suitable word in the Hebrew language at his disposal.'[25] Thus the historical consecutive account of creation in Genesis portrays God as above and outside his work, because he pre-exists and transcends creation (Ps. 33:6–7). Young says, 'The first verse of Genesis therefore stands as a simple declaration of the fact of absolute creation.'[26]

Darwinism denies completely the Bible's view of origins, rejecting the whole notion of a Creator and an eternal God. An acceptance of a theistic-evolutionary hypothesis may be an endeavour by some Christians to remain in the mainstream of things scientifically but it has the effect of undermining the Bible as the inerrant Word of God, fully reliable in fact and doctrine. Theistic evolution refuses to accept the Bible's clear and timeless account of creation in six days, giving credit to non-scientific theories which are biblically absurd. If the Bible cannot be trusted from the very first verse (when it comes to origins), how, then, can it be trusted when it comes to the great matters of the soul and eternal life? To attempt to destroy the clear testimony of Scripture and keep its message from the people is the devil's work.

Chapter 8

Notes

1 **Alister McGrath,** *The Dawkins Delusion* (London: SPCK, 2007), p. 8.
2 Quoted in **Douglas F. Kelly,** *Creation and Change : Genesis 1:1–2:4 in the Light of Changing Scientific Paradigms* (Fearn: Mentor, 1997), p. 17.
3 **Richard Dawkins,** *The God Delusion* (London: Transworld, 2007), p. 138.
4 *The Times,* Thursday, 28 February 2008.
5 **Kelly,** *Creation and Change,* p. 29.
6 'Does Science Make Belief in God Obsolete?', at: templeton.org/belief; **Tim Hames,** 'Does Science Make Belief in God Obsolete?', *The Times,* Monday, 26 May 2008.
7 **Bill Bryson,** *A Short History of Nearly Everything* (London: Transworld, 2004), p. 27.
8 Ibid. pp. 27–28.
9 Ibid. p. 37.
10 Ibid.
11 **J. A. Pipa** and **D. W. Hall,** (eds.), *Did God Create in Six Days?* (White Hall, WV: Tolle Lege Press, 2005), pp. 58–66.
12 **Louis Berkhof,** *Systematic Theology* (London: Banner of Truth, 1971), p. 29.
13 See **A. W. Pink,** 'Creation and Restoration', in *Gleanings in Genesis* (Chicago: Moody Press, 1950), pp. 9–19. This was not Pink's best work. It was written while he still accepted Dispensationalism.
14 **Ken Ham,** 'What about the Gap and Ruin-Reconstruction Theories?', in **Ken Ham et al.,** *The New Answers Book* (Green Forest, AR: Master Books, 2007), p. 47.
15 **Pipa,** 'From Chaos to Cosmos', in **Pipa** and **Hall,** *Did God Create in Six Days?,* p. 152.
16 Ibid. p. 161.
17 Apologetics is 'the use of theology in order to justify Christianity before men, in the claims it makes to be the ultimate truth, in the demands it makes on its followers, and in its universal mission', **R. S. Wallace,** 'Apologetics', in **J. D. Douglas,** (ed.), *The New International Dictionary of the Christian Church* (Exeter: Paternoster, 1978), p. 56.
18 **Mark Van Bebber** and **Paul S. Taylor,** *Creation and Time* (Gilbert, Arizona: Eden Communications, 1995), pp. 10–12.
19 **H. N. Ross,** *Genesis One: Dinosaurs and Cavemen* (Reasons to Believe, 1989).
20 The post-creation, pre-Fall covenant of work was made on condition of obedience so that Adam and his posterity would continue in the state in which he had been created.
21 'Naturalism has become the *modus operandi* of the secular scientist in our day. It is the guiding principle to which virtually all secular scientists adhere', **Tim Chaffey** and **Jason**

Lisle, *Old-Earth Creationism on Trial* (Green Forest, AR: Master Books, 2008), p. 118.

22 Don Stoner, *A New Look at an Old Earth: Resolving the Conflict Between the Bible and Science* (Eugene, OR: Harvest House, 1997), pp. 131–137.

23 Ibid. pp. 173–177.

24 E. J. Young, *Studies in Genesis One* (Phillipsburg, NJ: Presbyterian & Reformed, n.d.), p. 2.

25 Ibid.

26 Ibid. p. 7.

Conclusion

When Moses asked God his name, God replied, 'I AM WHO I AM' (Exod. 3:14). As Henry Law notes, this is significant regarding his eternal nature: 'If there had been a moment when His being dawned, His name would be, "I am what I was not." If there could be a moment when His being must have end, His name would be, "I am what I shall not be." But He is "I AM THAT I AM."'[1] God is not created, nor can he be destroyed, so we must begin with him. He is above and outside his creation, but Darwinians cannot believe this and, as a result, they suggest another reality. There are two ways to view the universe: one is to believe what has been given to us from its Maker and recorded in the inerrant Bible; the other is to follow the theories of the origin of the universe and mankind that are postulated by others whose worldviews are contrary to the Holy Scriptures and which, as a result, are in need of constant modification.

Two worldviews

Christian worldview	Atheistic evolutionary worldview
Begins with God	Begins with nothing
Based on the Bible	Based on man's present understanding of the universe.
Upholds the Bible's message	Undermines the Bible's message
Trusts the Scriptures	Human reason is the final authority
Keeps God in the system	Removes God from the system
Seeks to obey God	Is glad to reject God's Commandments
Sorry to disobey God	Rejects the notion of sin

Notes

1 **Henry Law,** *The Gospel in Exodus* (London: Banner of Truth, 1967), p. 14.

About Day One:

Day One's threefold commitment:

- To be faithful to the Bible, God's inerrant, infallible Word;
- To be relevant to our modern generation;
- To be excellent in our publication standards.

I continue to be thankful for the publications of Day One. They are biblical; they have sound theology; and they are relative to the issues at hand. The material is condensed and manageable while, at the same time, being complete—a challenging balance to find. We are happy in our ministry to make use of these excellent publications.

JOHN MACARTHUR, PASTOR-TEACHER, GRACE COMMUNITY CHURCH, CALIFORNIA

It is a great encouragement to see Day One making such excellent progress. Their publications are always biblical, accessible and attractively produced, with no compromise on quality. Long may their progress continue and increase!

JOHN BLANCHARD, AUTHOR, EVANGELIST AND APOLOGIST

Visit our website for more information and to request a free catalogue of our books.

www.dayone.co.uk

Evolution: good science?
Exposing the ideological
nature of Darwin's theory

DOMINIC STATHAM

160PP, ILLUSTRATED PAPERBACK

978-1-84625-170-2

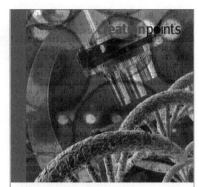

Evolution:
Good Science?
Exposing the ideological nature
of Darwin's theory

Dominic Statham   DayOne

Darwin's theory of evolution is often presented as scientifically proven fact. Few are aware, however, that there are serious problems with the theory. We are only told about the evidence that appears to support it, yet many scientific observations seriously undermine it.

Using plain English, Dominic Statham explains the main arguments presented by evolutionists and reveals their major flaws. He shows that much of the scientific data is actually consistent with a biblical account of creation and gives readers confidence to hold fast to the Bible as the true revelation of God, his creation and his dealings with mankind.

'... an excellent summary of the origins debate. Dominic Statham is well qualified to take on the task of analysing a mass of disputed evidence and making conclusions that are fair and justified.'
STUART BURGESS, PROFESSOR OF DESIGN AND NATURE, UNIVERSITY OF BRISTOL

'I enjoyed this book very much! I recommend it to anyone interested in the origins controversy.'
DR R. TERRY SPOHN, PROFESSOR OF BIOLOGY AND ASSOCIATE DIRECTOR OF CREATION STUDIES, LIBERTY UNIVERSITY, LYNCHBURG, VIRGINIA, USA

Dominic Statham is a chartered engineer and graduate of Loughborough University. He has twenty-five years' experience in aeronautical and automotive engineering, with Rolls Royce (Aero and Industrial & Marine Divisions) and GKN, a leading supplier of automotive driveline components. His recent vehicle projects include Land Rover Discovery 3, Freelander 2 and the Jaguar XF. He has extensive experience of both manufacturing and product development, and holds a number of patents.

STUART BURGESS

32 PP.

978–1–84625–100–9

creation points
IN GOD'S IMAGE
The divine origin of humans
Professor Stuart Burgess

Humans have great physical, mental and spiritual abilities that are far beyond what is needed for survival. This 'over-design' provides compelling evidence that man was specially created as a spiritual being. This booklet describes the following unique characteristics of humans:

- Unique upright structure
- Unique skilful hands
- Unique fine skin
- Unique facial expressions
- Unique language and speech
- Unique childhood
- Unique marriage and birth
- Unique brain
- Unique beauty
- Unique genome
- Unique spirituality

The booklet also discusses the origin of man and the purpose of human life from a biblical perspective.

Stuart Burgess has taught engineering design at leading UK universities. He has also carried out spacecraft design for the European Space Agency. In 1989 he received a Design Council Prize for engineering design presented by the Minister of State for Trade and Industry. In 1993 he received the Turners Gold Medal for engineering design presented by the Vice Chancellor of City University.

Creation & Evolution
Why it matters what you believe

COLIN GARNER

32 PP.

978-1-84625-099-6

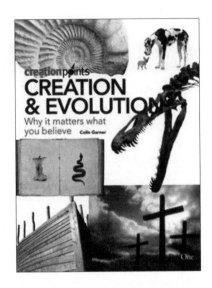

Why is the creation/evolution issue so important? And hasn't science disproved the biblical creation account anyway? The world's evolutionary view permeates virtually all society and secular science, and many people, even Christians, hold an evolutionary view almost by default. They reject the biblical creation account in Genesis as fact. In this booklet Colin Garner demonstrates that, as well as being inconsistent with biblical truth, evolutionary theory has serious fundamental scientific weaknesses. He highlights the reasons why Genesis, the first book of the Bible, is of such foundational importance to life today, in the hope that it will encourage us all to base our beliefs, our evangelism and our hopes on the whole Bible, including its vital foundational teaching on creation.

Colin Garner PhD is professor of applied thermodynamics at a leading UK university. He conducts research for the UK Government and several major international engine, vehicle and fuel companies. His research has been featured in *New Scientist* and he has presented his work on national BBC TV and radio. He lecturers on creation/evolution at the East Midlands School of Christian Ministry. Colin is married to Sue and they have three children.

Hallmarks of design:
Evidence of design in the natural world

STUART BURGESS

256PP, ILLUSTRATED PAPERBACK

ISBN 978–1–846251–39–9

Hallmarks of design

Evidence of purposeful design and beauty in nature

Stuart Burgess　　　　　DayOne

The Design Argument contends that design in nature reveals a Designer. *Hallmarks of Design* presents this in the light of the latest discoveries about the complexity and beauty of the natural world. Features of the book include:

- Six clear hallmarks of design;
- Over thirty diagrams;
- Description of how the earth is designed for mankind;
- Description of the Creator's attributes

Dr Stuart Burgess is Head of Department of Mechanical Engineering at the University of Bristol. His research areas include the study of design in nature. He previously worked in industry, designing rocket and satellite systems for the European Space Agency. He is winner of the Worshipful Company of Turners Gold Medal for the design of the solar array deployment system on the £1·4 billion ENVISAT earth observation satellite.

'Compelling presentation of the evidence of design in the natural world.'
—*BANNER OF TRUTH MAGAZINE*

He made the stars also:
What the Bible says about the stars

STUART BURGESS

192PP, ILLUSTRATED PAPERBACK

ISBN 978–1–846251–20–7

This book teaches clearly and biblically the purpose of the stars and the question of extra-terrestrial life. Dr Burgess explains how the earth has a unique purpose in supporting life and how the stars have a singular purpose in shining light on it. He explains why the universe contains such natural beauty and how the stars reveal God's character.

Dr Stuart Burgess is Head of Department of Mechanical Engineering at the University of Bristol. His research areas include the study of design in nature. He previously worked in industry, designing rocket and satellite systems for the European Space Agency. He is winner of the Worshipful Company of Turners Gold Medal for the design of the solar array deployment system on the £1·4 billion ENVISAT earth observation satellite.

'Dr Burgess has a very clear style and his book brims with interesting material. It will be greatly appreciated.'
—DR PETER MASTERS, METROPOLITAN TABERNACLE

'Both our world and the heavens seem to sparkle with a new identity as a consequence of this book.'
GEOFF THOMAS

'There is a great need for a book which gives clear biblical teaching on the purpose of the stars and the question of extra-terrestrial life. This book meets that need.'
CREATION SCIENCE MOVEMENT

The origin of man

STUART BURGESS

192 PP PAPERBACK

ISBN 978-1-903087-73-2

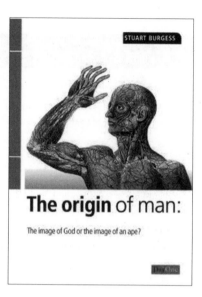

The origin of man:

The image of God or the image of an ape?

Have humans descended from apes or was man specially created? Do humans have unique characteristics and abilities that set them apart from all the animals? The answers to these crucial questions determine whether man is just an animal or a special spiritual being. This book shows that there is overwhelming evidence that man has a Creator. The book has many diagrams and includes explanation of similarities between humans and apes, unique characteristics of humans, unique beauty of humans, archaeological and fossil evidence and the importance and relevance of the origins debate.

Dr Stuart Burgess, BSc, PhD, CEng, MIMechE, is a Reader in Engineering Design at Bristol University. His research areas include the study of design in nature. He previously worked in industry, designing rocket and satellite systems for the European Space Agency. He is winner of the Worshipful Company of Turners Gold Medal for the design of the solar array deployment system on the £1.4 billion ENVISAT earth observation satellite.

PHILIP SNOW

240PP ILLUSTRATED PAPERBACK

ISBN 978–1–846250–02–6

Birds are amongst the world's most beautiful and beloved creations, so it is unsurprising that they have been so widely studied. This book examines closely their wonderful aerial lifestyle and unique, warm-blooded design—often so different from the cold-blooded dinosaurs that they are claimed to have accidentally "evolved" from! Especially as they often precede dinosaurs in the fossil record and their miraculous genetics, as ours, speaks of special Creation—not random "Big Bangs", chance chemical soups and endless genetic mistakes! They have been carved and painted since earliest times, on rocks, temples and associated with pyramids and religions art and literature, sport and farming, war and peace and even Heaven and Hell.

Philip Snow is a wildlife and landscape painter, illustrator and writer. His work appears in many publications and galleries and he has illustrated, or contributed work to, over sixty books and many magazines, prints, cards, calendars, reserve guides and decorated maps etc. Publications include several Collins guides to UK and European birds, and paintings have been exhibited in many top galleries, in the UK and abroad. Latest books (2005) include a Hebridean

Design and origin of Birds

Day One

Wildlife and Landscape Sketchbook, several Children's Biblical colouring books, a book on estuary life and migration and regularly exhibitions of paintings and prints.

Philip Snow has produced a unique book which expertly describes and illustrates the design, life and beauty of birds.
STUART C BURGESS, PROFESSOR OF DESIGN AND NATURE, UNIVERSITY OF BRISTOL

**Genesis for today
The relevance of the creation/
evolution debate to today's society**

ANDY MCINTOSH

240PP ILLUSTRATED PAPERBACK

ISBN 978–1–84625–051–4

Professor McIntosh is a scientist who sees no contradiction between science and the events of creation in the book of Genesis. He believes that all Christian doctrine, directly or indirectly, has its basis in the literal events of the first eleven chapters of the Bible, and that these foundations of the faith are being undermined in the church by the fallible theories of evolution.

'For those who have eyes to see, here is ample proof that God's revealed truth is as trustworthy as ever—and infinitely more certain than every human speculation.'
—*JOHN MACARTHUR*

ANDY MCINTOSH

Genesis for today
Showing the relevance of the Creation/Evolution debate to today's society
'Genesis **IS** for today'—JOHN MACARTHUR

THIRD EDITION

WITH NEW CHAPTER: 'GENESIS AND THE 21ST CENTURY'

Day One